MIXED
BLESSINGS

MIXED BLESSINGS

WILLIAM & BARBARA CHRISTOPHER

Abingdon Press

Nashville

MIXED BLESSINGS

Copyright © 1989 by Abingdon Press

This book is printed on acid-free paper.

Christopher, William.
  Mixed blessings.

  Includes index.
  1. Christopher, Ned—Mental health. 2. Autistic
children—United States—Biography. I. Christopher,
Barbara, 1934— . II. Title.
RJ506.A9C46 1989 362.19'8928982'00924 [B] 88-7860
ISBN 0-687-27084-7 (alk. paper)

ISBN 0-687-27084-7

MANUFACTURED BY THE PARTHENON PRESS AT
NASHVILLE, TENNESSEE, UNITED STATES OF AMERICA

For
Ned and John

CONTENTS

INTRODUCTION

I have had the good fortune to be part of one of the most widely acclaimed and popular comedies in television history. The experience of making television is not nearly as glamorous as it might seem, nor are the actors involved a particularly glamorous group of people. Yet there is a certain aura of glamour which comes with show business success, and a certain number of honors that are the by-product of it.

That is how it happened that on a particular evening in early 1987 I stood at a podium, blinded by lights, being applauded for my contribution to the image of religion on television. My thirteen years of playing Father Mulcahy in "M*A*S*H" and its sequel "AfterMASH" had not turned me into a priest, and I hope that it was with humility that I accepted a statuette that seemed more appropriately to belong to a fictitious character. There was little I could say about religion to an audience that knew a great deal more about it than I did. Instead, as I accepted the award, I spoke about my real-life experiences as the father of an autistic child and the awareness I had come to of the needs of the handicapped in our society.

Unknown to me, a representative from a publishing house was in the audience that night, and he thought that the story of an actor and his family and their struggles with the devastating handicap of autism would make a book. Some weeks later I heard from my manager. "I've received an interesting phone call," he said. "How would you and Barbara like to write a book about your life with Ned?" Write a book? That sounded like a lot of work. In my career I had been content to rely on other people's words; on film and on stage I had always had expert writers to put words into my mouth. What's more, a book about our family seemed particularly challenging—and somewhat intrusive, for we could not possibly tell Ned's story without revealing a great deal about our personal and private life.

My first inclination was to say no. But through the years I had received considerable mail from parents of handicapped kids telling me how it comforted them to know that I shared their problems. Perhaps in telling the details of our experiences we could help other parents who were embarked on the voyage of frustration and discovery that life with a handicapped kid ensures. Perhaps, too, in telling Ned's story, we could bring about a greater general awareness of the puzzle that is autism. We consulted John, our older son, told him of the offer we had received to write a book about his brother, in which he, of course, would play a considerable part. "I think you should do it," he said.

That is how we came to write this book. Having said yes, we then were faced with the task of reconstructing the last twenty years, and trying to do it as accurately as possible. There we ran into some good luck. Barbara's mother had not only kept all of her letters, she had also made extensive notes of telephone conversations that related to Ned's problems and had kept those. She had kept John's letters too, which gave another point of view on the passage of those years. This was a start on recalling it all. We dug out the old diaries, the letters from physicians, the school and therapy reports, the photo albums. We laughed at forgotten memories and disputed over details imperfectly remembered. Occasionally, we were overwhelmed with sadness at the anguish we uncovered in the record of those years. But mostly we were struck with the sense that our problem was only a problem; that every family has something to contend with and somehow we had managed to have a lot of fun along the way. John summed it up, commenting, "Ned was my brother; it was my life; I thought it was normal."

William Christopher
Pasadena, California
June 25, 1988

CHAPTER 1

Certainly Different

T here's no oleanders out there," remarked Ned as he stared out the window in disbelief at the snow-filled swimming pool. We were in Winnipeg, happy as clams and feeling very lucky. Our little family was all crowded together in a one-room apartment, and who really cared if the temperature outside was thirty-nine below zero. It was the year of the maxi-coat. I didn't need one in Los Angeles, but a three-month stay in Canada gave me the excuse I needed to be fashionable. Bill was working in a play—the happiest of conditions for an actor, a good part in a good play in a wonderful theater. John, our four-and-a-half-year-old, had survived a recent brush with meningitis without any damage, and Ned, two years younger, was newly toilet-trained. An occasional letter from our old friend Harry, who had agreed to take care of our house while Bill worked at the Manitoba Theater Center, told us all we needed to know about Los Angeles. We could get almost half of the network news from New York on television, along with lots of "The Dick Van Dyke Show" and Jack LaLanne and, of course, "Sesame Street." And maple butter could be had at a reasonable price at the nearby store.

Winnipeg not only had a great theater, it had a great zoo, a fact of almost equal importance to us, for we were very much in love with being parents. We braved the weather on daily outings, congratulating ourselves that our children were not, after all, going to grow up in the softness of Los Angeles without ever experiencing the character-building northern climate. It would take us forty-five minutes to suit up, only to

—11—

find that Ned's recently acquired training forced us to start all over again. The children and I caught pneumonia for a while, but our bodies revived and so did our spirits. There were no playmates but ourselves, and we learned to live closely together and like it.

We played in the snow, and if we had any nagging doubts when Ned cried as he was placed on the sled, we dismissed them and carried him or let him trudge alongside. He was only two and a half, but he was a sturdy walker. We brushed aside our doubts, just as we had back home when we took him for a Christmas portrait. He had cried so hard as the photographer put him up on the stool that he finally had to have his portrait done standing up. The photographer hadn't liked that at all. All the other children always sat on the stool without complaining, it seemed. We brushed aside our doubts, just as we had when I took Ned for his first haircut and out afterwards for an ice-cream soda. I had done the same with John two years earlier, and it had been wonderful fun. But Ned couldn't sit at the counter without setting up an awful wail. Abandoning the sodas, I lifted him down, gave him a hug, and took him home. It had not been much of an outing. He certainly was different from John.

Now when Bill tried to piggyback him after the sled didn't work out, Ned protested mightily, stiffening his back and making piggyback impossible. "Did you ever hear of a kid who didn't like piggyback?" said his frustrated father. No, he didn't like piggyback, just as he hadn't liked being cuddled when he was a tiny infant. He hadn't liked it, and he had stiffened his little body into a board, making it impossible to cuddle him. But we had persisted and made a game of tickling and rubbing him into a more babylike shape, and at times he did come to enjoy it. Maybe he would come to like piggyback and the sled. We would keep trying. And he was showing so many new skills.

Ned's new abilities included writing the letters of the alphabet, rather odd, square-looking letters but clearly distinguishable as the ABCs. He was learning to dress himself, and he had acquired a burning interest in flags. No one flies more flags than the Canadians—national flags, provincial flags, visiting flags. Ned grew to love them all and to know them all. He sat on Bill's lap as we rode the buses around Winnipeg, and although we were somewhat exasperated when he repeatedly slid off, stiffening his body again, we put it down to the unfamiliar and slippery snowsuit. He looked out the window, exclaiming at the sight of every flag, demanding to know its name. He didn't ask in words or the kind of words we should have expected. He shouted out, "Flag!" in a piercing voice, and looked excited. Bill understood what he wanted and told him the names of the flags, hushing him when his exclamations grew too loud for public consumption.

Back in the apartment we watched with pride as Ned struggled to dress himself. We tried to comfort him when he raged at his inability to put his underpants on right and raged even further when we tried to help. How terribly independent he is, we thought, when he insisted on his own struggles. Finally, inspiration struck, and I said, "The label goes in the back, Ned." And he understood. Problem over, we thought. What other two-and-a-half-year-old was that smart? Bill brought home flag books, and Ned expanded his knowledge. He soon was saying, "That's Yugoslavia!" "That's Botswana!" as well as, "That's Manitoba!" as Bill pointed to the flags. He didn't respond to the landlady's "What's your name, little boy?" but then she had a Russian accent. "Is he all right?" she asked us. Of course he was all right.

He was absolutely beautiful. Blooming cheeks and the bluest eyes and a fit, muscular body. He looked wonderful in the darling little suits my mother loved to send him. Ash blond hair, thick and straight and somewhat coarse, a contrast to his brother's bonny brown hair and eyes. And a contrast, too, to John in his language. At Ned's age John had been chattering away for months. The courage to plunge ahead with our complex and beautiful language never failed him. Sentences and vocabulary, concepts and questions, imagination and variety—these we had seen fully displayed by wonderful John. Ned could comment accurately on the lack of oleanders in Winnipeg; he could learn the flags; but he couldn't tell the landlady what his name was. Ned was certainly different. But he was entitled to that, wasn't he? And besides, look at how he could write and dress himself and amuse himself.

Amusing himself was another new skill. Ned had never shown much interest in toys. His Manitoba flag was the first toy he really loved, and when we bought him a beautiful set of painted wooden blocks, he was delighted. He built intricate structures, carefully executed according to some plan that existed in his own mind, selecting colors and shapes very carefully and making extensive layouts across the room. These blocks were quite tiny, and his care and precision in handling them was wonderful.

At night, when Bill left for the theater and the children fell asleep, I would settle down with Jane Austen and read of another society where people lived closely together and had to make a series of adaptations to that closeness. Our children were as different asleep as they were awake. While John slept peacefully, Ned rocked. He would get up on all fours and rock back and forth rhythmically by the hour, sound asleep all the while. We knew he rocked at home—sometimes he would rock his crib all the way across the boys' room—but living with the rocking night after night in one room did make us very aware of it. We didn't know of any other children who rocked in their sleep, but it didn't worry us too much. It made some kind of sense that such an active person would be active asleep or awake.

After two months in Winnipeg, or "Winterpeg" as John, with his gift for words, called it, Bill trouped to Vancouver to another theater to continue performing the role of Willy Mossop in *Hobson's Choice*. The climate was better but life was much the same as it had been. Each night Bill got ready for the theater and went off to perform, leaving the rest of us to entertain ourselves. There were afternoon expeditions with the kids to beautiful Stanley Park or to the beach to climb on the logs that wash up on the shore in such abundance. I made occasional forays into the nearby shops—perhaps a walk to the bakery to buy a Battenburg cake, or "Batman" cake as John taught Ned to call it.

CERTAINLY DIFFERENT

March 25, 1971
Vancouver, British Columbia

Dear Mother:

I just got home from shopping. I tortured myself for hours in a knit shop until I realized that I haven't even finished the sweater I started two years ago and by the time I do I'll have worn out my knitting enthusiasm for five years more. I compromised and bought Bill a dark brown Aran knit cardigan. There was a special on them at Hudson's Bay Company and I am sure he'll love it—when he gets home from the playground, that is. (John and Ned aren't going to want to give up Daddy as a playmate when they get home.)

I won't be writing again from Canada. Tomorrow and Saturday I'll be busy getting ready to leave, and Sunday morning early, we're off! We will be home around April 1.

You asked again for the boys' sizes: John 5, Ned T4. I don't have any ideas about clothing for them as it's so long since I've seen their wardrobes. They are getting big tho' and John is just about past the cute little suit stage. He starts kindergarten in the fall, you know. He likes very soft, comfortable things and can handle just about any fastenings. Ned is about the size that John was when you saw them at the Christophers'. He isn't fussy about what he wears. He is crazy about flags and has been for about six weeks now. He is learning all the flags of the world, so if you see anything with a flag motif, he will love it. He is not on a bottle. He is a "big boy," toilet-trained and almost always dry at night now. (Thank heavens!) I have ordered him a bed like John's and hope it will be there when we get home. However, he probably wouldn't mind the crib for a while as he is so tired at night that he's practically asleep when he hits the bed. That's because he never stops running. What stamina!

They just came in from the park. Bill says they haven't sat down since 10:00 A.M. (now 4:00 P.M.) except for lunch! Neddie loves "Sesame Street" now and will sit in front of the TV until dinner time.

Speaking of which, I have to get to work!

Love to you both, B.

Yes, we were challenged by, but rather proud of, all that activity and stamina. In Bill's family there has been a tradition of giving each child a "word." Bill's was "Cooperation," and when our kids came along, John was dubbed "Reliability" and Ned "Determination." We laughed at how apt these epithets were for them.

So we set off home again, driving down the Pacific Coast. Our kids were seasoned travelers by this time, and they enjoyed the drive. (Returning to the United States was something of a disappointment to Ned—not enough flags!) We had missed the Los Angeles earthquake, and by the time we returned, a spilled jar of jelly, the only casualty, had run down the entire inside of the cupboard.

Ned seemed a bit lost as John resumed his old life, nursery school, and friends. We puzzled over how to keep him happy and hit on the idea of school for him too. He was younger than John had been when he had started school, but then John was so social and always had lots of friends around. Ned's solitary state no longer quite pleased him, and so we enrolled him in the Christian Nursery School, the school where his big brother was so happily occupied.

And how did he do? He built awfully tall towers with blocks and created amazing structures around them. He demonstrated, to anyone who would ask, his great knowledge of the flags of the world. He parallel-played with the best of them. His teachers said that he was the smartest little boy they had ever seen but that he didn't play with the other children. But we weren't to worry about it; he was young in his group and many little children do not know how to interact with their peers, especially those who have had most of their contact with adults. "He's certainly not at all like John."

No, he wasn't. He turned three, and the interest in flags was still very much alive.

Studio City, California
May 21, 1971

Dear Mother:
I have been terrible about writing, I know. I don't even

remember the last letter I wrote you! First of all, we had so much yard work to do. Everything had grown up so much in our absence. We have pruned the pittosporum at the side of the house way down so that we have much more light in the living room. I have done away with living room curtains entirely. I can't face making new ones and the old ones are gone. It looks cool and the shrubs give us enough privacy.

Of course I had to get my vegetables going. Tomatoes, beans, peas, snow peas, eggplant, lettuce, peppers, squash, cucumbers, pumpkins, cantaloupe. All doing well so far except peas.

The boys' birthdays were great. (Did I write about John's?) John wants to wear his safari shorts every day and berates me if they aren't clean. The bathing suits are adorable and have been in the sprinklers but not to the beach.

Neddie's birthday should be renamed flag day. The miniature flags went on the cake and on the cupcakes for school. He was very excited and impressed everyone with his knowledge. He is doing well in school—enjoys it and the teachers think he's great. Talking quite a bit now although he is still frustrated by his inability to express himself fully. He needs to catch up to himself. The bird shirt and the blue shorts are very cute on him, the sunsuit too.

We have had the usual deluge of New York visitors, and Liz and Lou and their little boy arrive from Philadelphia day after tomorrow. Will be here a week. I am excited about seeing them, but we will be pretty cramped in this house.

With all of this, we haven't been further than Pasadena in our new car. But it is great! And it's wonderful to have a car of my own as it is so hard to work around Bill's schedule. He is shooting a commercial today for Grapefruit Tang, a new product. The TV season should be starting soon and with luck there will be work then.

I keep thinking that if Bill could get a good bunch of commercials going at once we might be able to buy a house. And the house in Pasadena that our friends Suzie and Mark live in (I have always loved it more than Suzie does, she tells me) is going to be on the market!

I have also been reading a series of articles in the L.A. Times about how difficult it is becoming to adopt infants. The waiting period has gone up to fourteen months from three at the time we got Ned. Of course we can't apply for a baby until we are ready (which we aren't). And really, a baby would mean moving (which we would like to put off with the idea of making our next move to a house of our own). These are just some thoughts, not problems, as we always look to The Fates to solve our dilemmas anyway.

No other news at the moment. Have to pick up my Little School Boy.

When are you coming to see us?

Love to Jim—and you, B.

As transplanted New Yorkers, we were enthralled with the opportunities that California gave us for gardening. We loved learning about the plants around us, familiar and exotic. And so did Ned. He was something of an expert in plants by this time. The garden of the previous summer had provided him with his first real spoken vocabulary. I had planted vegetables among my flowers and was so proud of them that I took every visitor on a tour, pointing out each plant. Our yard was very small and the garden was planted around the edges. Ned hadn't followed along as I pointed out my plants, but he must have been paying attention because suddenly he began to do the same thing. He would toddle around the garden naming eggplant, tomato, and green beans. He had just turned two, and he knew all the plants in our yard that he had ever heard the names of, not only the vegetables but the shrubs. We were amazed. And what is more, he could identify all the plants he knew wherever he saw them. On our walks about the neighborhood he would call out, "Tomato!" "Eggplant!" "Pittosporum!" "Ligustrum texanum!" and point to a plant, while ignoring the nice neighbor who was saying hello to him. In our innocence, we called him our little scientist. He hadn't spoken much up to that point, just a very rare "Mommy" or "Night-night." The vegetables had given him the focus he needed to break the silence. We were so pleased—and yes, relieved.

Ned had an eye for foliage. One of his most frequent

observations was to classify the plants in offices and public places with a seemingly critical "Artificial!" or more rarely, an approving "Real!" Bill had taught him this distinction when he noticed Ned fingering a plastic plant in the doctor's office, clearly aware of the difference between it and the real thing. When we saw the chance to teach Ned a concept that would help him over a hurdle, a vocabulary word that would clarify something that puzzled him, we would always provide it. But more often we didn't know what he was working on and were surprised when a whole body of information would appear that we knew no one had ever taught him. On the awful day John came down with meningitis, I had absolutely thrown Ned at my neighbor Leona, who happened to be circling our quiet block on her bike, saying, "Take care of him. We have to get John to Children's Hospital right away." It was ten days before I saw Ned again, but I was in touch with Leona from the hospital.

"Do you know he can count?" she asked.

"Yes," I said, "I think he can count to ten."

"Ten! He can count to forty!"

He was just a little more than two years old and no one had ever taught him. He didn't need to be taught, he just learned.

Perhaps we had a genius on our hands. At nursery school he heard "Twinkle, Twinkle Little Star" played on the piano by Mrs. Higby, and again Ned did not express his interest directly. But when we visited Leona, he went to her piano and tried to play. Lots of kids do that, of course, but Ned wasn't satisfied with the sounds coming out, and he stayed at the piano until he had picked out the tune. There was some anger and frustration as he tried and failed, but he was determined. I did point out middle C to him. (Was this "the label in the back" again?) I began to think I could see how he learned, and it certainly was not the way John learned.

And colors—he was interested in knowing the names of the colors. I had designed and silk-screened a color book for him, but he was soon beyond its limits. He wanted to know all of the colors: magenta and dark blue, cerise and light blue. Sitting in the bath, he lined up his plastic nesting cups along the edge of the tub, saying, "That's dark blue. That's light blue." Then after a puzzled pause, "That's just blue." There was another pause and he repeated, "That's dark blue. That's light blue. That's ___ ?"

"Medium blue, Ned," I provided.

"That's medium blue."

He noticed subtle differences and wanted the words to cover them, or at least understood that there was a vocabulary to describe his observations. But the everyday words and everyday communication didn't appear to interest him.

We lived in a very friendly neighborhood. Joe Finnigan would drive slowly down the street on his way home from work, waving to the children and calling, "Hi, John."

"Hi, Mr. Finnigan."

"Hi, Kirstin."

"Hi, Mr. Finnigan."

"Hi, Matthew."

"Hi, Mr. Finnigan."

"Hi, Ned . . . The only kid on the block with an unlisted number," said Joe.

With all of his learning of categories, vegetables, flags, colors; with all of the great pleasure he demonstrated in his buildings, rushing into the kitchen to get me ("Show Mommy!"); and with all of my reports to my mother that he was talking "quite a bit now," he still wasn't really talking, wasn't talking the way John had. He just didn't seem to hear strangers when they spoke to him. He readily responded to us and even used sentences, but aside from the rare brilliant observations ("There's no oleanders out there") that sometimes came out of him, they weren't quite like the sentences other kids used. He said, "What's that?" for "Who's that?" and, "You want some juice?" meaning "Can I have some juice?" More often, he relied on scraps of sentences to cover his needs: "That's a ___?" when he wanted to know the name of anything, or, "Have that?" when he wanted to be given something. He had a limited number of constructions that he formulated for use in a broad variety of situations. Once he found a sentence that worked, he stuck with it without variation. His vocabulary kept increasing as he demanded more words, but the new words were mostly nouns, labels.

It was summer. School was over for a few months. John was out riding his bike with his friends. Ned was playing "Twinkle, Twinkle, Little Star" on Leona's piano. John was pretending to be a fireman or a cowboy. Ned was building with his tiny blocks, balancing them perfectly. "He's a little bit different," said my other neighbor, Theresa.

Studio City, California
August 19, 1971

Dear Mother:

We are continuing to have the heat wave to end all heat waves! The temperatures are in the 90s but it is very, very humid. Very unusual for L.A.—in fact, this is the first for us in over seven years here. (Can it be!) Even the nights are hot. I really long for a swimming pool.

My neighbor Theresa just moved to a larger house nearby with pool and when we were there last week Ned surprised us all—most of all himself—by swimming or rather wriggling across on his own. He has no fear! I decided that since I can't trust Ned that I had better get John water-safe so that when I visit our pool friends I can devote more attention to Ned the Dauntless. So I started John on swimming lessons, and he's fantastic! He can already belly-flop into the pool and swim to the instructor, swim underwater, and is learning to float. I don't really think Ned is teachable yet but may learn on his own.

Ned is having his usual kind of troubles. I took them to the dentist for checkups and he was found to have four cavities! Two of them may require root-canal work. It has been an ordeal for us all, especially the dentist, as Ned is one of those on whom tranquilizers have either no effect at all or the opposite effect. Ned puts up quite a struggle but doesn't suffer any after-effects and is perfectly willing to go back and likes the dentist. He does seem to be one of those people for whom nothing is easy.

We have been silk-screening another book—Bill's story, John's drawings, a scribble by Ned—my lettering and layout. A true family venture.

I know I had many things to tell you but all goes out of my mind with the constant interruptions for juice, sprinklers on, potty seat on, sprinklers off, etc.

Out of town guests next week. I lied and said we couldn't accommodate them here, but they have written back: "Can we camp in your driveway?" I give up.

Would love to see you and Jim. Letters are so hard to write.

Love and kisses, B.

It did seem very odd that a three-year-old had cavities in all four molars and root-canal work to be done in two. The dentist said something about a possible malformation in those teeth before birth. Of course, tranquilizers didn't work on Ned; he would be impossible to tranquilize—all that zest for life. It was strange that he became overexcited and drunk-seeming on a medication that was supposed to make him sleepy; but the root-canal work got done with a lot of patience on everyone's part and a bag of flags to amuse Ned with, and we trusted that he would never need to be medicated again or that he would outgrow this strange reaction as he had outgrown his other "usual troubles." He had worn a splint on his leg as a tiny infant. There had been something not quite right in the way his feet turned, but of course, it had been corrected, and now he could walk and run perfectly. He had walked before his first birthday. He was running soon after and hadn't stopped since. Just look at how vigorous he was. He hadn't laughed or smiled responsively until he was three months old. But we had explained that by his eye problem. He had been slightly cross-eyed, and we had taken him to the Jules Stein Eye Institute at UCLA. When the doctor put drops into his eyes as two of us held Ned down ("Strongest baby I've ever seen!" said the panting doctor), Ned became able to focus. He suddenly laughed, and I cried. I didn't even know I had been worried until that moment and I didn't learn much about myself either, because here I was three years later still not acknowledging my worries.

Studio City, California
September 13, 1971

Dear Mother:
Well, school has begun! John, as could be expected, marched

into kindergarten as if he had done it thousands of times before. He is very assured and takes to new experiences easily.

By the way, he is taking his swimming very seriously. He continually practices (on dry land) his breathing rhythm. I was pleased to see him work so hard at it, as real effort was required and he has always found everything so easy. Now when we go to a pool he swims back and forth, very serious and determined. He looks like a little seal when he comes up for air, brown hair all slicked down and big brown eyes blinking. Very cute!

As for Ned—he is taking nursery school in stride. He feels very at home in the situation. I am glad that we gave him a few weeks of it during the spring. Now he can feel like an old hand. He is astounding in his abilities. He is learning Greek and Hebrew letters. He still knows all of the flags. He can spell about fifty words and recognize them when he sees them. Of course life is still a challenge with him. His latest is "playful" slapping, which NOBODY likes. I hope he will be over that by the time we see you. Maybe school will help. His teacher is marvelous and understands him.

The big news here is the weather. The worst is over and it was the worst ever: 120 degrees, believe it or not, for three days, down to 95 at night. Absolutely impossible! Worse than Winnipeg at minus 39. We kept wishing that we could move out toward the ocean.

Speaking of moving, Mark and Suzie have bought a new house and their old one is now available.

More later. How about news of you?

Love to Jim, B.

Within a month we were busy buying the house in Pasadena that I had been dreaming of. We could hardly believe our luck: a house with three bedrooms and a beautiful big back yard on a very nice street with lots of kids in the neighborhood. We were in touch with the Los Angeles County Bureau of Adoptions. We were going to have room in the new house for another baby, a girl this time, and as we knew the wait would be long, we thought we had better get started.

We were spending a lot of time at the new house cleaning out the overgrown garden, making repairs and plans. To familiarize the boys with the area, we took walks around the new neighborhood, occasionally hiking down into the Arroyo Seco, a large wild area running from the mountains to downtown Los Angeles. As it passes through Pasadena the Arroyo is a park, and our new house was actually on its slopes. There we could glimpse California as it used to be, the Pasadena that attracted settlers from the Midwest a hundred years ago, with its wild canyon and the scent of chaparral and orange blossoms. In one short block we could be within the park. It was a retreat from the demands of the new house and a place vast enough to absorb all of Ned's energy. We knew we were doing the right thing to move to Pasadena to this wonderful neighborhood.

Ned had a new passion. He loved signs. The stop sign was his very favorite. When he discovered that "STOP" occurs in the middle of "CHRISTOPHER," he would letter his name and draw an octagon around "STOP" with a vertical line extending downwards. This drawing delighted him, and he did it over and over again. I made him a stop-sign costume for Halloween, and Bill bought him a set of miniature traffic signs. Ned carried them around with him almost as much as he did his flags. He could read them all. He would stick them in the ground and then run past them looking over his shoulder like a football player. He would run to the stop sign at the end of the street and circle round and round it. The other kids would try to join him. "Use words, Ned," I would say to him when he pushed them away. He's just got some little private game he wants to play, I guess, I would say to myself.

And then there was hair. He loved hair. He loved to touch the part in my hair. He loved to touch the hair of the little girls at the Christian Nursery School. "Ned is the smartest little boy we have ever had in this school, but he is not relating to the other children except to put his hands in their hair, and sometimes he even pulls it. We would like to have some professional advice so that we can help him. We're worried about Ned, and we know you are too."

Feeling a little stunned, I got on the phone to UCLA to track down a psychologist. "I am having difficulty with my little boy. He is three and a half and can't seem to relate to other children. His nursery school asked me to get some help. He seems to be very bright, but he becomes fascinated with certain things. Right now it's hair, and he is pulling the hair of the little girls in school." One after another they responded with some variation of "Oh, a behavior problem. I'm afraid I don't have time for that kind of problem in my practice." Until one of them finally said, "I can give you the name of someone who might be able to help." Relief. I had lost three valuable days in trying to help my wonderful but puzzling little boy. I had no time to waste.

Ned and I were off to see Dr. Danielson. I was nervous but optimistic. He, after all, might be able to help us. He listened to my history of Ned and of his school problems. He observed Ned and asked him some questions. He watched and listened as Ned repeatedly tried to touch the part in my hair and then experimented with pulling my hair. "No, no, Ned," I said firmly, "I can't let you hurt me." I looked at the doctor, smiling at this perfect demonstration of the school problem I had been describing. The doctor looked seriously at me.

"Mrs. Christopher, your little boy is retarded. School is just too much for him. I advise you to take him out at once. Take him home and love him. There is nothing else you can do."

"What do you mean, retarded? Why, he can name all the flags of the world. Did you ever meet another three-and-a-half-year-old who could do that? He could do it before he was three!"

"I'm afraid he has been pushed."

"We certainly never pushed him!" I protested. "He's the one who insisted that we teach him. It started when we were in Canada, and he developed this consuming interest in flags."

"But flags can have no true meaning for him. It's just rote learning."

I didn't continue to argue, but I knew full well that Ned knew the difference between Canada and the United States. Canada was that place with all the wonderful flags. And at home we had the occasional Stars and Stripes and the California flag.

And it was a lot warmer here. That's pretty good geography, I thought, for a little kid. And besides, even if the flags weren't truly meaningful . . . How much did flags mean to Dr. Danielson, anyway? Can flags be truly meaningful? I wondered what this man thought about flags or if he did. I thought they were symbols for places and so, I supposed, did Ned. But I couldn't get into all that. And besides, there were lots of other things that Ned could do. Perhaps I hadn't made that clear to the doctor.

"Okay, maybe he doesn't understand the full significance of flags, but he taught himself to write. And he can name all the plants in our garden and can read the traffic signs. And what about the piano? At his school they think he's very smart. He builds wonderful buildings and . . ."

Ned and I left the doctor's office and drove slowly home. I called Bill.

CHAPTER 2

Getting Help

I was spending my days getting the new house in Pasadena ready to live in. As I began sanding a section of floor that Tuesday, my thoughts were on Barbara. She and Ned had an appointment with a psychologist to get some guidance for us and for Ned's nursery school teachers. After the initial surprise at their request, I had begun to admit to myself that they were being very sensible in asking for help. After all, they must be mystified by Ned, even though they were used to dealing with a great variety of kids. I'd like a few answers myself, I thought. I set to work with a light heart. I figured that with all Ned had going for him, a little guidance would get him on track in no time.

I hadn't been working long before the phone rang. It was Barbara, and she was crying. "Dr. Danielson says that Ned is retarded and that we should take him out of school."

"What!" Slowly I sank down on the dusty floor. "Did he say what to do about his hair pulling?" I asked. "And what about guidance on how we can get him to talk more? And how can he be retarded if the school thinks he's so bright, and what about all the things he can do?"

"I went over all that. According to Dr. Danielson, he is retarded and associating with all the normal kids isn't good for him. It will only frustrate him, and he'll keep pulling hair."

"And the flags?"

"He says Ned was only showing off for us and we must have been pushing him."

We talked on the phone together a long time. Then I locked

up the empty house, leaving the floor half sanded, and drove home to Studio City. We talked a whole lot more. We were confused by this diagnosis, and we also wondered about the doctor's recommendation that we take Ned out of school. But it was the only advice we had and perhaps we'd better follow it. Besides, we were about to move. We would settle into our new house, make it beautiful for our new life, and then do what we had to do to find the right path for Ned.

So we did take Ned out of school. They were sorry to see him go, and we loved them for it. A few days later, a big envelope arrived in the mail addressed to Ned. It contained good-bye cards from Ned's classmates, with their childish drawings and names printed at the bottom by the teachers.

"Indian!" Ned shouted.

"Well, maybe it's an Indian, Ned," I said doubtfully, "but it looks like a flower to me."

"Indian!"

I suddenly realized that the child's name was India and that Ned had read it. We went through the cards, Ned reading each name aloud. He had learned to read all of the names of the kids in his class, and no one had taught him that, I was sure. He couldn't be retarded. I knew that. Dr. Danielson just had to be wrong.

Glad to have something positive to focus on, Barbara and I turned our energies to the move. There was much to be done, especially in the garden. There would be ample room for flowers, vegetables, swing, climber, with plenty of space left over for someone Ned's size to charge around in and not feel crowded. But only if I got on with the necessary clearing, hauling, and digging. The hard work would be comforting.

We took the boys to Pasadena almost daily. Ned loved the flagpole that greeted us as we exited from the freeway at the top of Colorado Boulevard. It is a very tall pole and has a handsome bronze eagle at the top. Ned made up a little song about flagpoles: "Some have a point; some have a ball; some have an eagle." He had been fascinated by points for a long time: the points on the rose thorns in our garden, the points on the iron fences in Canada, the points on some of the toy flags he played with. His Manitoba flag had a ball, and the Pasadena flag had an eagle. Some have a point, some have a ball, some have an eagle.

We were doing a fine job, we thought, preparing a smooth transition. We made frequent trips to Pasadena. We met our new neighbors and the boys had a chance to mix with the neighborhood kids. We were sure the move would be fairly easy for them. But Neddie, who was usually so detached, and who had been dragged around Canada without protesting, was wary and upset. It was time to see the pediatrician for a regular visit, and we talked to him about all that had been happening.

"Ned has been having some problems in school and we took him to a psychologist and he says Ned is retarded."

"Ned retarded? Nonsense. You just have to look at him to see how bright he is." That was a relief to hear. We were glad to have someone else affirm our belief that our child was bright, but that dreaded word "retarded" still lingered at the back of our thoughts.

"We're going to be moving soon. And Ned seems upset. We've talked to him about moving and we've taken him to the new house over and over, but he is crying a lot more."

"Have you told him you are taking him with you?"

Well, no, we hadn't. Not in so many words. But surely he knew that. Well, maybe not. So we told him.

"Ned, we are all going to the new house together—Mommy and Daddy and John and you! And all of your toys—your stop sign, your Manitoba flag, your blocks and books, everything. And you will share the boys' room with John just as you do here. We are all going to be together." A miracle—he stopped crying; he understood. He was going with us to the new house. That would be just fine with him. We kept describing to Ned in detail what would happen on moving day, how we would all be going to live in the new house in Pasadena, showing him where his bed would go and where he could keep his little flags and blocks.

The move was accomplished early in December. The Christmas tree filled the empty corner of the living room. Barbara's mother, Betty, and her husband, Jim, flew out to admire our new house, and Jim hung a swing for the boys from our avocado tree. My parents sent some furniture and rugs from their attic, and we settled down to live in our new home.

The new year began with a flurry as it always does in Pasadena, when an extra million people arrive to view the Tournament of Roses. Ned distinguished himself at the rose parade by dashing out of the crowd to grab a flower off a float. "Chrysanthemum!"

Barbara was off to shop for curtains. She came home from her expedition without the curtains but with a positive and cheerful face. "Guess what happened? I was sitting in the tearoom at Bullock's, and I had to share a table with another woman. I always hate to do that, you know. I don't know what came over me, but suddenly I burst into tears. The woman finally said, 'All right, tell me about it. It can't be that bad.' And I did. All about it. Isn't it amazing how things turn out sometimes? She's a nurse who works for a neurosurgeon and she gave me some very good advice: 'Don't believe everything the professionals tell you. Use your own common sense. You know your little boy is not retarded. You also know there is something wrong. Call UCLA, the department of pediatric neurology; describe your son and get him over there for tests. Don't take no for an answer.' "

Barbara is a woman of action. She was on the phone to UCLA at once, and after talking to many people at some length, she finally got through to the department of pediatric neurology. The secretary was quite careful to discuss all aspects of Ned's development to make certain that we belonged there. We did, it seemed, and she made an appointment for Ned. We were confident that now help was on the way.

I would be the one to take Ned to UCLA. After her rather crushing visit to Dr. Danielson two months ago, Barbara wasn't eager to go through it all over again. Besides, it was my turn. It is a principle of our life together that we share the work. I remember my father saying to me on the phone the day that John arrived in our lives, "I would never trust a man who wouldn't change his baby's diaper." One of the advantages of an acting career is that it gave me time to be with my kids and to be involved with the whole childrearing process.

The waiting room at pediatric neurology was very large, with child-size tables and chairs. There were quite a few kids, all with at least one worried parent, usually the mother, who was either standing or squeezed into one of those little chairs. The tables were spread with puzzles, toy cars, blocks. It was evident that most of the children had something terribly wrong with them. Some lay about limply, some had tantrums, some cried. It was very noisy. I couldn't really belong there, with my beautiful, healthy little boy. Sure, he was different, but he wasn't like these children at all. No one could think that these kids were normal. The strain of being there was enormous, and every part of me objected to the specter of being the parent of an abnormal child. But I wanted answers. This was 1972; this was UCLA; this was where you came for answers.

"Why isn't the mother here?" asked the doctor.

"She took Ned to the last doctor. We thought it was my turn," I said.

"Oh?"

Apparently he wasn't used to dealing with dads. The doctor took a complete history of Ned. When did he roll over? When did he sit up? Fortunately, I had brought the notes that Barbara and I had made together. What were his first words? (Would he believe "green beans," "tomato"?) Then it was time for some tests. Ned had a physical; he had an X ray, some kind of brain scan; he had an EEG. We went home to await the results.

Ned and I went back to pediatric neurology a few days later, and this time I found the waiting room experience easier. I felt lucky my little boy was as well off as he was; but looking around at those other children, I realized that they were just children. True, they weren't much like Ned and even less like John, but I began to see them all as children and not outside my world.

There were three doctors present at this second session. Two of them looked on while the third, Dr. Phelps, said to me, "Call Ned over to you, please." I was puzzled but I did so. Ned responded as I knew he would. Then Dr. Phelps tried. "Ned, come over here." Nothing. Then the doctor made a loud noise with a couple of pieces of wood. Nothing. "Whisper to him," he said.

"Hi, Ned," I whispered. Of course, Ned looked around.

"You see, no problem with his hearing," the doctor

pronounced, turning to his colleagues. I could have told him that. Ned could hear the cookie jar being opened from the farthest reaches of the house. Then the doctor took me aside and summed it all up. "Atypical with autistic features. He should be in a special school as soon as possible. There is one run by a prominent psychiatrist you could look into. Please bring Mrs. Christopher with you for our next meeting." So Ned should be in school and as soon as possible. The last doctor had said to take him out of school. I was glad that Barbara would be with me the next time.

Barbara wrote to her mother about our final visit at UCLA.

Pasadena, California
February 22, 1972

Dear Mother:
The yard is looking beautiful. Peaches and apricots are blooming, also violas and narcissus. The lemon tree is in bud and the scent of spring is wonderful.

Not much news about Neddie. The EEG and X rays showed no abnormalities. I asked Dr. Phelps what he means by atypical and he said, "Atypical means he's different and we don't know why." I didn't like Dr. Phelps—very cold—never spoke to Ned, kept referring to him as "the case." He feels that Ned should be in a therapeutic nursery school, but the suggestion he gave Bill on the last appointment was for a "psychiatric preschool," which has no openings until September. When I told him that, he questioned (mind you, he was the one who suggested it originally) whether Ned could benefit from a program that is psychiatrically oriented and then suggested UCLA's school (also full), which is behavioristically oriented. But he didn't really make a definite recommendation. When I asked, he said we would have to decide for ourselves. All rather unsatisfactory. What are we supposed to base that decision on? We are confused and sometimes I wonder if we have done the right thing in putting Ned and ourselves through all this. I'll keep you informed.

Meanwhile, Ned is making great strides: has learned to swing on his new swing standing up and on the old swing (quite tricky—the single rope one), is riding trike and kiddie car.

Things have settled down to normal between the boys and they occasionally play together. He is writing quite well too. Oh, well—I'm sure we'll resolve this.

With love to you both. Write soon. B.

Barbara and I had had our final conference at UCLA, and it was over. Now where were we? Dr. Phelps had said there was nothing wrong. Well, not exactly nothing wrong, but nothing that could be measured, nothing that could be seen. He had said "a special school." He was very clear about that. As he put it, Ned was a perfect candidate for such a school. But he hadn't been any help in finding one, and when he said we would have to make the decision on what kind of special school, I felt he wasn't doing his job. After all, he was the expert, the professional. What did we know about special education? We weren't even entirely sure what special education meant. We had been counting on something to go on, direction, guidance. Of course, I was glad to know that our son didn't have a brain tumor or anything terrible like that, but I felt very frustrated that we still had no definite course of action for helping him.

Barbara was feeling equally impatient and, as usual, was quick to act. She was on the phone to a school for atypical children.

"How did you get the number," I asked.

"I just looked in the Yellow Pages," she said with a rueful smile.

We laughed. The Yellow Pages were not exactly in my genes, but they were certainly in my history. My father had made his career in Yellow Pages advertising. There was a kind of justice to this. What UCLA had failed to do, the Yellow Pages had provided. Barbara and Ned had an appointment that same week.

Pasadena, California
March 9, 1972

Dear Mother:
I was just sorting clothes and folding the cute trail shorts and shirts you sent the boys. John will only wear very soft shirts,

tender morsel that he is. Ned HATES buttons on shirts. Otherwise anything boyish pleases them. Ned still enjoys the flag motif and can now manage snaps, zippers, belts, etc. Dress-up seems to be out. John went to a birthday party last week and refused to dress up. He said that at the last one he went to he was the only boy dressed in short pants. He was right.

I am working in house and garden today—beautiful day, and we are going to visit Leona and Bob tonight. They were married on Sunday in Las Vegas. Leona has given Ned her piano (baby grand, old, very pretty) as Bob already has one.

As to the news about Ned. I am finally on the right track and have found someone helpful. I took him to a school for atypical children for an interview. The woman was great. She played, roughhoused, talked, laughed, deliberately frustrated him, etc. In twenty minutes she had seen all of his moods and had established true rapport with him. Her analysis: He shows some symptoms that are seen in autistic-atypical children but to a very mild degree. His language is slightly behind but not seriously. He is responsive, has good cognitive skills, good motor development. She feels that special education is not indicated. She had some concrete suggestions about handling him and about his education. She also cautioned against overreacting on our part. She feels we should just continue to investigate medical reasons for his problems. She said "a complete, sophisticated, medical workup by a specialist in child development" should be our next step. She recommended such a specialist, a Dr. Jane Salley. I have made an appointment April 4 with Dr. Salley and her office outlined their procedure: first, a complete physical, subsequent psychological testing, and a final session with both parents to discuss findings, plan program, etc.

I am feeling very relaxed now as I am sure we will get some answers. And, of course, I am relieved to have someone give an opinion on Ned that is quite reassuring, especially as I feel it came out of an understanding of him as a person rather than a "case."

Much love, B.

PS Love to Jim too. The swing is great.

Life in the new house was taking shape. Barbara planted an herb garden and I laid bricks. Our street, lovingly known as "Diaper Alley," was crawling with kids, and John joined the gang. Ned tried to join the gang. He tagged along and we were pleased to see what we felt was very appropriate social behavior finally beginning to show itself. But then he began to get rebuffed. He might have fooled an onlooker, but he couldn't fool the gang. He just didn't speak their language. The other kids approached him, puzzled. What kind of a kid is this, anyway? It wasn't long before Neddie was left behind, and he began spending much of his time constructing his elaborate layouts. He had little baskets of blocks and plastic letters that he lugged about the house, selecting just the right location. The carefully planned arrangements that he had begun in Canada had become amazingly complex, sometimes extending from his room all the way across the house to the kitchen. At the perfect spot in his mental plan, he would reach into his letter basket with two hands and grab just the right letters to spell NED CHRISTOPHER, JOHN CHRISTOPHER, WONDER, LIFE, TIME. Our walls were covered with the brilliant pop-art serigraphs of Sister Mary Corita. Barbara had studied with her for four years, and we had slowly acquired quite a good collection of Corita prints. Words from the worlds of advertising, supermarkets, magazines, products were displayed in large, bright letters. WONDER, LIFE, TIME.

If anything happened to disrupt his layouts—the "gang" dashing through with John, "Hi, Ned"—Ned would patiently pick up all the little pieces, the blocks and letters, the toy cars and plastic dinosaurs that he added to his design (not as cars or dinosaurs but as mere shapes in his plan) and start all over again. Sometimes what he made was so beautiful and had taken him so much painstaking time that we left it in place, carefully stepping over it. But when the moment came that we said, "Time to put your toys away," Ned didn't mind. He destroyed his design. There were plenty more where that came from.

Barbara wrote to our old friends the Seabergs:

Pasadena, California
March 23, 1972

Dear Steve and Ronnog:

Your letter just arrived and I read it at once and now I am sitting here feeling quite forlorn. We really are too much out of touch! Bill always feels that he is so close to his old friends that he doesn't really have to write letters, or at least that is his excuse. He isn't here to defend himself as he is off in Colorado shooting a commercial.

Last year was very busy for Bill despite what is a full-fledged depression in Hollywood. When we returned from Canada he did a recurring role on a TV show, "Nichols" (now canceled), plus three appearances doing improvised comedy on "The Carol Burnett Show."

The children are growing up (to no one's surprise). John (almost six years old now!) is in kindergarten and gets himself to and from school on the school bus. He is very social and enjoys himself. He has occasional crushes on girls and mopes around saying things like, "Why don't you wear red bows in your hair, Mom?"

Ned, almost four, is an unusual person. Life with him is difficult and interesting. He is enough of a challenge to us that we have shelved our idea of adopting a little girl. Perhaps we will wait a few years and adopt an older child. We will have to see what develops. Ned needs a lot of attention and love and patience. He is almost antisocial and plays by himself or with us. We have moments of worrying about him and times when we think he is a genius. Life was and still is quite simple with John. Well—it's difficult to describe the children as the words are no sooner on paper than they have changed.

Oh, dear! It's hopeless to write letters.

We must see you.

Love, Barbara

We took our troublesome genius to see Dr. Salley. Barbara went with him for the first appointment, and Dr. Salley and Ned hit it off right away. He responded well to her warmth and friendliness and he liked her; he usually did like pretty women. The appointment was a very pleasant experience for him, not at all like UCLA. "No UCLA!" "No Dr. Phelps!" were exclamations that we would be hearing for years.

Dr. Salley gave Ned a thorough physical and administered a variety of tests. She took hand prints, explaining that since hands develop at the same time as the brain, lines in the hands can indicate disease. She checked his vision and hearing. She tested him to rule out diabetes and brain damage. She took a complete and detailed history. When did he roll over? When did he sit up? Barbara described his behavior as an infant—how he had stiffened his body, how he had dug his tiny fingers into our arms, how he had had trouble sucking the bottle, how he hadn't begun laughing until three months, how he had been afraid of unstable situations, how we had had to work so hard to get his attention sometimes.

Barbara came home with a lot of news about the visit and the doctor's preliminary ideas of where Ned stood in the four major areas of child development. Dr. Salley had said that Ned was about a year behind in gross-motor development—walking, running, jumping. She found his language to be within normal limits, and even very advanced in vocabulary. We were rather surprised at this assessment but it had been a particularly good day for Ned's language. When he first arrived at the office he looked up at the clock on Dr. Salley's wall and announced, "The clock is broken." She was amused and agreed with Ned. Later he had hurried into the room where Dr. Salley and Barbara were talking and interrupted with, "Look Mommy, I have seven yellow cylinders." It was one of those occasional bursts of very normal language that always amazed us. He was right, of course; geometric shapes were another of his categories, and he had found seven yellow cylinders among the blocks in Dr. Salley's playroom.

Dr. Salley had sat Ned at a desk and had him build, write, and draw (fine-motor work, as we were learning to call it). Except for a slight immaturity in the way he used his hands, he scored very high in this area.

In the fourth area, that of personality and social development, Ned had what Dr. Salley called a scatter—sometimes okay and other times like an eighteen-month-old. He couldn't communicate with his own age group because his immaturity was getting in the way. He was gifted in intelligence, not mentally retarded, but his gift was not going to do him any good unless he was helped.

Dr. Salley also assured Barbara that she wouldn't leave us high and dry; that if she suggested a school, she would see to it that Ned got in. Before making her final diagnosis, Dr. Salley would read all the previous records from UCLA and Dr. Danielson and would review her initial findings to determine where she would have to test more intensively; then she would develop a program for Ned. This all sounded very encouraging. Here was someone who would really help us and who saw Ned as the wonderful little person he was.

Pasadena, California
June 8, 1972

Dear Mother:
My birthday gift from the children and Bill is two baby ducks! They are supposed to control the snails in my garden "organically," but meanwhile they are more trouble than the snails. They have to be kept warm, can't get wet, must come in at night (in a box) for three months! Cute, tho'. They are terrified of us but not of the children, which goes to show how smart they are. I hope we all live through the experience—including the ducks.

Regarding Mother's Day: No, my boys didn't remember me. I woke up with an earache; later Bill was pruning a tree and sawed off a branch that hit my sore ear, and while I was consoling myself by playing the piano, John's bike was stolen. I guess I wouldn't mind something a shade more sentimental than that!

Ned and I have seen Dr. Salley a second time, and Bill and I will be meeting with her next week to set up a program for Ned and to discuss her findings. Briefly: She retested him without my being present and concluded that he is less slow in the motor area than she had thought and just as bright as she had thought and better adjusted socially. In essence his problems are milder than she originally felt. She had suggested him for a new federally funded preschool program but now seems to feel that he is "too normal" for it. I am anxious to have our meeting and get going on something for him. But it won't be long now! More another time.

Love to you and Jim, B.

Barbara and I had our conference with Dr. Salley and the results were certainly encouraging. Prognosis excellent. Ned was a healthy child with no physical handicaps or disabilities. There was the possibility of a biochemical imbalance too subtle to be picked up by modern techniques, but Dr. Salley said that new methods of scanning blood and urine were being developed at a rapid rate and might prove useful in future. We thought ourselves lucky to be living in such a scientifically advanced age.

Dr. Salley ran through all of her findings that day, and at each point we found ourselves reassured and comforted; nothing sounded particularly hard to deal with. Ned's eye problem from infancy had not been completely corrected and might be contributing to his present difficulties. It was not serious, however, just something that should be checked regularly. He might have to wear glasses when he was older.

Although Ned's hearing was perfectly normal, there was something wrong between the auditory information going into his brain and what was coming out. This indicated that the central nervous system was the problem. That made a lot of sense to us. We knew Ned wasn't deaf, but we also knew that he responded strangely to sound, often overwhelmed by it, covering his ears with his hands, or heedless of it. And some of his speech sounds were a little strange; he had a broad *a*, for example, almost like an English child although we were most definitely Americans.

In the motor area his delay was not serious at all, just something we should remain aware of. He should not be urged to do things he wasn't ready for. He would eventually catch up.

Regarding that mysterious word "autistic," Dr. Salley was particularly reassuring. "He is *not* autistic. He does have some behaviors that might be found in an autistic child, like turning the lights on and off. Ned might do this for several minutes; but an autistic child would do it for hours. On the yardstick of autism, I would put Ned at the one-inch mark." She had discussed the results of her findings with Dr. Phelps, and he had agreed to remove the word "autistic" from Ned's records so that incorrect labeling would not follow him.

Dr. Salley's original impressions of Ned's intelligence had been borne out by further testing. In fact he scored very high, at the seven-year-old level in some areas. This was the confirmation we really wanted; we could not hear too often the opinion that Ned was not retarded. She said that his problems were in the emotional area. He didn't talk well because he didn't want to. Rather than dwell on why, we were to provide him with a program that she outlined for us.

We left Dr. Salley's office in good spirits. We had to get home and start making plans for Ned along the lines she had recommended. We would be getting him into a play group for the summer and setting up a combination of therapeutic nursery school and regular nursery school for the fall. Dr. Salley wanted Ned to have the benefit of the experts in a therapeutic school, but she emphasized that she wanted him to be with normal kids as much as possible. She didn't want him in contact with kids who were seriously handicapped or disturbed. He would need help to fulfill his potential, which was so high, but special school would not be necessary for long. He would definitely be in a regular kindergarten when he was five. In other words, a pretty normal schedule, with guidance.

Normal school by the time he was five! That was great news. Of course, Dr. Salley had said that if the proposed program didn't work out, there were other therapies we could pursue, but we were sure that wouldn't be necessary. The bills for all this investigation had at first seemed staggering, but now they were of far less concern. It looked as though we weren't really facing anything very serious. Only a year of special education, at most.

There was something else contributing to my feeling of well-being. My agent had just called, telling me to get out to Twentieth Century Fox for an appointment with the producers of "M*A*S*H," a new television series scheduled for the fall season. I was to read for the part of Father Mulcahy, an army chaplain. As I drove out to West Los Angeles, I felt especially optimistic. There had been a preacher in the family sometime in the nineteenth century, and perhaps this was my chance to carry on the tradition. My grandmother had always thought of me as a likely candidate for the pulpit. I had my fingers crossed that the producers of "M*A*S*H" would agree with her.

Pasadena, California
August 19, 1972

Dear Mother:

Just a note to get back in practice writing. No special news here.

*Bill is working on "M*A*S*H." This is his third show and he works again next week. He is very pleased with his part and with such regular work. I hope the show is a hit, as this could be great for Bill. I suppose we will know by the end of September. Of course, he has no guarantee, but the producers seem to like his work. I wonder how well a war setting will go over with the public at this time. Everyone is so very sick of Vietnam.*

Ned has not begun his special school as yet but I expect him to do so in a couple of weeks. He will go five mornings a week to the Fisher Clinic, a therapeutic nursery school, and three afternoons a week to a regular nursery school. Meanwhile he is playing in the park two hours a day with two older children. This was Dr. Salley's idea to give him a "life of his own." It is working well and I think he enjoys home more and is playing more with the neighborhood kids. He is an expert trike rider now and very daring at climbing.

John has learned to do the crawl and can ride his bike very well—no hands, etc.—but I think summer vacation is wearing a bit thin. It's three weeks until school begins and we are all quite ready.

*Our fall schedule will be really something. John will have to leave for school at 7:30. Ned will have to be driven to both schools and I am hoping to take a landscaping course at the arboretum. I also want to get back to silk-screening. We expect Bill to be working on "M*A*S*H." Well—I am looking forward to all of it, especially Ned's schooling.*

Much love to you and Jim, B.

PS The ducks are flying.

CHAPTER 3

Magic Mirror

Fall arrived. Ned started at the Fisher Clinic, and it was a new way of life for us. There wasn't time for the landscaping course at the arboretum that I wanted to take. There wasn't time for much. Part of the Fisher program was for parents to learn from the professionals by observing them work with the children through a "magic mirror." Our presence was required daily; at least mine was, for Bill was working at Twentieth Century Fox and couldn't be there every day.

The parents would sit in a tiny, crowded, airless room and stare at their little ones through the one-way glass. The children sat on the floor for rug time just as they do in a normal school. The teacher had cards with everyone's name printed in large letters:

"What does this say, Ned?"

"N-E-D—Ned."

"No. Just say 'Ned.' "

"Just say Ned."

"No, Ned, look at the card. What does it say?"

"N-E-D—Ned."

"Ned!"

"N-E-D—Ned!"

Well, he *had* been dubbed "Determination."

The name cards had a circle of construction paper pasted on them, a different color for each child. Ned's card had a circle of what had once been red paper but which had faded to a dusty pink.

"What color is this, Ned?"

"Pink," he declared.

"No, it's red," stated the teacher. Then she repeated her question. "What color is it?"

"Pink," he replied.

"No, it's red."

"No, it's red," he echoed.

The teacher tried again. "What color is this, Ned?"

"Pink."

I was muttering to myself by this time, "But it *is* pink! Stick to your guns, Ned!" I was an artist and I ought to know, I thought. And Ned knows too. What's wrong with these people?

"What color is this, Ned?"

"Pink."

"No, it's red."

"No, it's red."

He would echo this magic phrase because he understood something was wanted by the teacher but he was certainly not going to admit that pink was red. He was also echoing her speech because, we were told, he was "echolalic." This was a new term we were learning. It meant he sometimes repeated the words and phrases that others had uttered.

Bill and I were increasing our vocabularies greatly. There was a whole body of language to describe little kids like ours who were having difficulties with the world. "Aphasic"—that, according to Bill, who is a longtime student of Homeric Greek, ought to mean "no speech." But that didn't describe Ned at all. He had a lot of speech, albeit not perfect speech. But aphasic, it seemed, did apply to Ned. Aphasic children had trouble with language; they had "communication disorders."

Trouble with language—we knew Ned had that. Not only was his language unusual, he had moments when it didn't work at all for him. For example, he was waking in the night, crying for the door to be open:

"Can I open the door?"

"Sure, Ned, you can open the door."

"Can I shut the door?"

"Yes, Ned," his tired father said. "The door can be any way you want it. But we all have to go back to bed."

"Can I open the door?"

"It *is* open."

"Can I shut the door?"

"Yes, if you want to."

And so on until we were all thoroughly awake and all thoroughly upset with each other.

This was quite a problem. "Whatever are we going to do?" I asked one of the therapists. This was happening night after night, and it was beginning to tell. The young woman, a "trainee" (not strictly a jargon word but one I grew to dislike very much because it usually meant that inadequately trained people were being asked to teach us about our child, in fact, to train themselves on him) had a suggestion: Why didn't I get out paper and crayons and have him draw pictures?

"What! At two in the morning?"

"Yes, this sometimes helps disturbed children."

"You have to be kidding. I have another child to get off to school at 7:30 A.M., and Bill has to be at the studio at the crack of dawn sometimes. I just can't get up and have an art session in the middle of the night."

She looked at me and sighed.

"Can I open the door?"

A few sleepless nights later I had an inspired thought. "I know what the matter is, Ned," I said. "You are afraid of the dark. You want me to leave the hall light on." That was just what he wanted. He trotted peacefully back to bed, the tears not yet dry on his face. This was what was meant by aphasic.

Aphasic. At least we had a label to apply to Ned. Dr. Salley didn't want Ned called autistic, and neither did we. That was a terrible word, we had come to realize. Autistic kids were strangely withdrawn; they loved spinning objects; they liked to turn lights on and off by the hour or do any number of odd things by the hour (this, we learned, was "perseveration"). Autistic really meant self-involved, said Bill, but whatever it really meant, it was used to describe a group of children who were in big, big trouble.

As we sat crammed in behind the magic mirror, an occasional observer would join us. One of the staff would bring the visitor in and begin to discourse on the problems of the children, or "clients," or "cases." The term "functionally retarded" came up over and over. I deeply resented having my child discussed with a stranger in my presence without introduction, and I particularly disliked hearing him called anything I didn't sanction. I was getting tired of explaining that Ned could do a lot of things and that I didn't think he should be called retarded.

"Look at me, Ned," the teacher would say when she greeted him in the morning. She held his chin until he gave her "eye contact."

"Good morning, Ned."

"Good morning, Ned," he would echo.

"No, say, 'Good morning, Sandy.' "

"Good morning, Sandy." But by this time the all important eye contact had slipped.

"Look at me, Ned." It would begin all over again.

Rug time was interminable. Not every child in the class gave the teacher a hard time over the names of colors, but they all had their own individual problems. They all had their worried parents sitting in the booth squirming through the morning. There were times when I thought the children would never be allowed to get up and run around.

They had their table work, and that didn't go very well either. With one swipe of his arm Ned would push the glue pots and construction materials onto the floor, relishing the annoyance he was able to provoke in his therapists.

Three days a week after the therapeutic school, we took Ned directly to the Calvary Presbyterian Nursery School (Mrs. Jordan's school, as Ned insisted we call it), a normal, garden-variety nursery school with a group of twenty-five normal kids and two teachers. Mrs. Jordan was a large, motherly woman with a deep, friendly voice. She had those kids in the palm of her hand. She loved them all. She gave each of them special attention, and when she wanted to give group instructions she sang. "It's time to put your toys a-way," she would sing. "Ev-er-y-bo-dy get off the swings and go in-to the class-room." And they all did as bidden, even Ned. He didn't have any trouble hearing Mrs. Jordan. Her singing directions communicated perfectly. She didn't demand that he look her in the eye. She knew pink from red. "He's a remarkable little boy," she said, and she called him "my Ned." It was like a breath of fresh air to see him in the utter normalcy of this setting. Ned followed along with the other kids; he played in the sand; he painted; he was a champion on the swing. He was admired for some of his accomplishments: He could count backwards from ten; he could tie his shoes (Bill had guided his hands only once and from that moment on Ned could do it himself); he could walk backwards; and, of course, he had his flags. He was doing well in this normal group. Mrs. Jordan accepted him; the kids accepted him.

We asked Mrs. Jordan to come and observe Ned's therapeutic school and give us her opinion. She did. "Those people don't know what they're doing. Who ever heard of keeping a group of four-year-olds sitting on the rug for an hour? I'm supposed to learn from them—hummph!" We pretty well agreed with that, but these were the experts who were supposed to be helping us.

"M*A*S*H" had debuted in September to very good reviews and had a certain prestige among our actor friends. The ratings had been only so-so, but everyone involved was proud to be affiliated with a "quality" show. It was our wedding anniversary the final day of filming for the season, and we had theater tickets for that evening, but we went to the set first for the "wrap" party. (Every business has its jargon.) We sat in the mess tent and enjoyed the feeling of success, the pizza and jocularity. When we had to leave early, Alan Alda walked us to the door of stage 9. "Well, this is good-bye for now," he said. And then with sudden concern, "What if the show isn't picked up? What if we never meet again?" Actors tend not to count their chickens.

The weeks and months dragged on at the Fisher Clinic. Bill was now with me daily, and we sat in the narrow room staring through the glass at Ned. Things weren't getting any better. Several of the therapists had long, swinging hair, and it was just too much for Ned. "Ouch!" and "No, Ned!" the girls would shout. And Ned would laugh.

Every single day we drove home on the Pasadena Freeway critiquing the morning session:

"Why on earth don't those girls tie up their hair? Don't they have any common sense?"

"It's just ridiculous to create situations that Ned has to be penalized for."

"I know. I know. It's incredibly inappropriate to have him go on pulling hair when the solution would be so simple."

"I hate it when he laughs after being so wicked."

"So do they."

We finally declared a moratorium on discussions about the Fisher Clinic in front of Ned. And we decided to have no Fisher/Ned rehashes after dinner. We had to set limits for ourselves. We had to be careful to stay in the normal world.

Sometimes Ned would laugh without such an exciting reason. Sometimes he laughed for no reason at all. We learned to call that "inappropriate affect" (accent on the first syllable). "Well, I'd rather have them laughing for no reason at all," said one of the mothers, "than crying for no reason at all." I wasn't so sure about that. The meaningless laughter made me feel so excluded. Private grief was something we were used to; people did sometimes cry when they felt sad, even when those around them didn't know why, but to have someone laughing and laughing for no apparent reason was eerie.

We were learning about something called "behavior modification" or "behavior mod." This was a system of rewards, called "positive reinforcers," for good behavior, with the objective of eliminating undesirable behaviors and creating compliance. This seemed to mean m&m's all morning long. "Help!" I said. "Any mother knows better than that. I don't give my children candy. Why, I even make whole wheat birthday cakes, for goodness' sake."

"Mrs. Christopher, you sound as if you expect the whole world to revolve around Ned."

"No, not really, but I do think that his therapy ought to revolve around him."

We were sitting behind the one-way glass, and I left the room for a moment. When I came back, Bill was white. One of the trainees had punched Ned in the chest and knocked him off his chair. This young man had flowing locks, and Ned had found his hair irresistible. We complained and were told that it certainly would not happen again; punching the children was certainly not part of the program. And besides, Scott, the trainee, had problems of his own. "Let Scott's mother worry about that!" I said. We were overreacting, we were told; in fact, we were too critical of the program in general. We were advised that if we wanted to get help for Ned it would behoove us to be more accepting. We should not be setting ourselves up as knowing as much as the professionals. Professionals don't like that. And when we left the Fisher Clinic we might find it hard to find a program if we were too exacting in our standards.

Oh, dear. I had not really meant to hurt anyone's feelings. I knew that everyone working there, including the trainees, really wanted to help the children. I was just baffled by what I observed every day. I didn't understand it, and most of all I didn't think Ned was getting any better. Oh, perhaps he was making progress in some areas; he was getting language therapy, and we thought he was improving in his use of prepositions. But he didn't appear closer to normal in the overall picture.

It was excruciating to sit in the booth and watch as a screaming Ned was held upside down. This was a "negative consequence," a term used to describe what we would have called punishment in a more normal world. But perhaps we had better not be too demanding. Where else had we to turn, after all? These were the experts. They were supposed to know how to help kids like ours. We had to give it a fair trial. We would try to be more accepting.

Another part of the program was the parent group. Here was a word I thought I knew the meaning of, "group." But in psychological terms this means group therapy, and the apparent object of this "group" was for everyone to cry. Well, I didn't want to cry. I didn't want to "share my feelings" with a bunch of strangers. I wanted to know what to do about my wonderful and beautiful little boy to help him get on track. He was supposed to be going to normal kindergarten the following year, and he wasn't getting closer to that goal. True, he was doing well in Mrs. Jordan's school, but there was no denying he was different. Our experience raising John had taught us what a normal four-year-old was like, and we knew Ned was very far from that, and he seemed to be getting farther.

Perhaps, we told ourselves, we were making a mistake in measuring Ned by John. John was so smart and capable. He had been tested and had qualified for the "gifted" program and was now, in the first grade, participating in a lot of activities that were supposed to enhance his "giftedness." Perhaps the contrast with John was just too great. Perhaps Dr. Salley was right, and Ned would be ready for kindergarten next fall. We kept hoping, but if it was only in contrast to John that Ned was so far behind, what were we doing at the Fisher Clinic? The kids there were all very handicapped. This was not a new word to us, but it was new in our thinking about Ned. Did we have a handicapped child on our hands, and what did that mean for his future, and ours, and John's?

Eventually, parents were asked to work in the classroom with the children. Professionals would sit at our elbows and tell us what we were doing wrong. We learned the correct speed for administering m&m's. We worked with the other children. Our hearts weren't really in that, but we did learn something about the group of children Ned was placed with, and we were terrified he might really belong there.

On the playground, Ned had begun to throw objects over the fence. Balls and blocks, twigs and leaves ("Magnolia!"), he lofted them neatly and watched them disappear, fascinated. We learned a word to describe this kind of behavior. It was called "stim." He had other "stims," like wiggling his fingers near his eyes, which he had been doing for so long we hardly noticed it anymore. And tearing paper, shredding it into tiny pieces and tossing them in the air to make "butterflies," as he called them. "Stim" is short for "self-stimulatory behavior." I rejected these jargon words as completely as I could. I preferred to describe what was going on rather than to label it. I would rather say "repeating words" than "echolalia," "throwing things" or "wiggling his fingers" than "stim." I would stick to the English language that I understood, I thought.

On our next visit to Dr. Salley, we poured out our frustrations about the Fisher Clinic. She told us their reports indicated that they considered Ned mentally retarded and severely emotionally disturbed. She didn't agree with that. They were attempting a therapy called interpersonal stimulation, which she felt was not necessary for Ned. They were considering play therapy, and she felt the benefits of that would be minimal. She was disappointed in the results of Ned's speech therapy, as he had not made much progress in spontaneous conversation. We agreed with all of Dr. Salley's points. We thought the Fisher Clinic was not doing anything very right, but she had sent us there, after all, and now despite all of her objections to Ned's program she wanted us to continue. However, she did want a second opinion, and she wanted it from a good, sound, medical person, a psychiatrist. This worried us. Our hopes had been so invested in the therapeutic nursery school approach. But unless Ned improved, he couldn't enter kindergarten in the fall. Dr. Salley still felt the prognosis was good.

"Is normal kindergarten still in the picture?" we asked.

"Probably," she said.

The psychiatrist wanted to meet all of us, so John went along too. Dr. Alexander was a very friendly man and spent quite a long time with us. He thought that we were handling Ned well and that John was wonderful. He explained that no one knew much about children like Ned. Although he wasn't particularly impressed with their work, he thought that we might as well complete the term at Fisher. He recommended that Ned continue at Mrs. Jordan's school and that he start working with a speech therapist who would help him develop his language and conversation. "The hope is that since Ned has high intelligence, with the right kind of speech therapy he will be able to use that intelligence to build his language strength." Psychotherapy was not indicated.

Eventually, the Fisher Clinic came to an end—not a minute too soon, as far as I was concerned. But I wept as we left. They had done their best; they were well-meaning people who wanted to help abnormal children get better. My tears were for Ned. He wasn't better, or not much better, not enough better.

At Dr. Salley's recommendation we were looking into a preschool program for aphasic children and trying to line up special kindergarten for the fall.

Pasadena, California
March 30, 1973

Dear Mother:

Just a quick note. But better than nothing, I suppose. Bill is in Atlanta! He flew yesterday evening and is shooting a commercial for an amusement park there—something like Disneyland. He is staying with the Seabergs and will be back on Sunday.

Ned finished up at the Fisher Clinic yesterday. There was a nice going-away party for him. I am very relieved to have this program come to an end. He didn't make the progress there we had hoped for and the strain of the schedule and the demands of Fisher were really too much for me. Now he is continuing his afternoon nursery school and is having two hours per week with a language therapist in a public preschool program. This will continue through the summer. In the fall he will probably attend a special kindergarten for children with language problems or, if his behavior hasn't calmed down by that time, a special kindergarten for educationally handicapped children. Each of the classes has six kids and two teachers; public school, transportation provided. We will be checking with Dr. Salley in two weeks and hope to start a vitamin therapy program at that time. So things are well mapped out for the next few months.

John is fine and he and Bill have joined Indian Guides, a Y program for boys and their dads. John's name is "Laughing Cloud," and Bill is "Talking Sky." The motto is "pals forever." John is SO excited! They are going on a weekend outing next month.

"M*A*S*H" looks good for next season. Keep your fingers crossed. Garden beautiful! I just heard about a low air fare in August. Maybe we will make it East this year. Fingers crossed again.

Much love, B.

Now that the Fisher Clinic was not in the picture, we resolved to be a more normal family. There was no point in trying to fix Ned while abandoning the life and standards that we wanted him to be normal for. Our financial situation had improved thanks to "M*A*S*H," and the show had been picked up for a second season. We took a brief vacation and went off to San Diego to stay in a resort hotel. Ned learned to swim underwater; he grew brown and even blonder in the sun. His "stims" looked more natural in this setting, and most of them were left behind when he had the excitement of new places and activities. On the beach he threw pebbles into the water, but so did most normal kids. We went off to Sequoia National Park for a long weekend and hiked through the stately trees. These were things that Ned could do as well as any normal child, and it made us feel more normal to do them as a family. This was much better than life in a glass booth watching someone give Ned m&m's or hold him upside down. We would never, we vowed, allow those remedies into our life.

Dr. Salley wasn't giving up either. She had some ideas about another approach that might help Ned.

Pasadena, California
June 27, 1973

Dear Mother and Jim:
We are having a very busy summer. Ned has nursery school three afternoons and language therapy four mornings and starts something new next week. It is a kind of occupational therapy using a sensory integration approach. This is a new idea, which I hope to be able to explain fully soon. We are going to see films and have the therapy explained at a meeting Thursday P.M. *Roughly, the idea behind this therapy is that Ned's sensory experiences are not processed properly. Therefore he has to figure everything out over and over again. He has to learn what he experiences rather than just reacting. So life for him is like a normal person's response to an optical illusion—you know what it is but not without using a thinking rather than a feeling process. I am very interested in this theory, as it seems to explain so much.*

Ned has been accepted into the aphasic kindergarten, or rather we are 99 percent sure of his acceptance. Only a formality remains. I am much cheered by all that is happening. I think we are on the right track.

John has summer school 8:30–12:30 daily. He is learning Japanese, Oriental cooking(!), drama and music, arts and crafts. After two weeks he switches to Spanish. Then one week of Swahili (! again). It's organized for fun with a one hour phys. ed. period and two recesses, so it's not too heavy.

Watergate, not to mention my incredible driving schedule, keeps me from accomplishing much. I tend to believe John Dean. What do you think?

Love and kisses, B.

My mother wasn't one to accept without question. She fired off a reply. What was this new therapy? Were we sure? Was it reputable?

Pasadena, California
July 10, 1973

Dear Mother:

Just got your letter. I really understand your concern but I feel that this approach is very reputable. It is occupational therapy but departs from traditional OT in using sensory integration techniques rather than activities for daily living, work skills, etc. We are enthusiastic but also pretty realistic. It may not work for Ned.

His therapist has demonstrated to us that Ned's reactions to motion and gravity are not normal. For example, when we roll John on a beach ball (a huge 60" one) he arches his back and lifts his head; he shifts his weight from side to side, trying to keep his balance. Ned doesn't do any of these things. He just lies there—possibly because he doesn't know he is falling or what to do about it. However in just a few days he has begun to react more normally. The theory is that the body can teach the brain to organize sensation. We take Ned to the therapist twice a week and follow through at home with motion activities and tactile stimulation. It is all fun for us and for him.

An example of an interesting difference in this approach:

Problem: Ned drinks milk from one side of his mouth. Answer, Fisher Clinic-style: Sharply, "Ned, drink like a big boy. Drink from the middle of your mouth." Result: He tries but soon reverts. More shouting. Ned becomes edgy. Milk spilled. Answer, sensory integration approach: Stroke cheek and side of mouth not being used, saying, "Where is the other side of your face, Ned?" or, "What's over here, Ned?" Result: Automatically corrects drinking.

Ned loves swinging. The Fisher Clinic said to limit him in this activity. Mary Silberzahn (Ned's occupational therapist) says he needs to experience "continuous motion through space." On a swing his body has to adapt in order not to fall off. He should be encouraged to swing as much as possible.

As you can see, this is a totally different way of thinking about Ned's problems, and I hope it will show results. I have been impressed by the therapist's ability to guess his traits and difficulties, particularly in areas unexplained by anyone else previously, for example, making patterns with toys and objects, tearing paper, digging in with his fingers, having difficulty drinking from a straw. As to how this affects behavior and sociability, the idea is that he currently needs to use all of his higher abilities to interpret sensations. His brain is so busy organizing that he has not developed the necessary skills to socialize, communicate, and monitor his behavior. Well, that's enough about that. Do you feel it is somewhat explained?

Love, B.

In a couple of weeks Ned had ceased to have difficulty drinking through a straw. Mary Silberzahn had instructed us to rub his lips with an ice cube wrapped in a cloth. We did this frequently throughout the day, and the extra stimulation did the trick. Soon he was drinking yogurt through a straw for practice.

In playful sessions in Mary's garage, Ned balanced, rolled, swung, rocked, and spun. In each of these activities she tried to get him involved and self-directed. "Self-direction is important to self-organization," Mary told us. In his favorite activity he rode on a "horse," a padded beam suspended on springs. He could sit on the horse and push himself or bounce. He could lie down and hug the horse with his arms and legs while Mary pushed him. At home we hung a hammock from the apricot tree with both ends tied together on one branch. Ned could swing himself, or we could swing or rotate him. Bill lined a barrel with carpeting, and we rolled it back and forth with Ned inside, then Ned had a chance to roll himself. We worked with him on the beach ball so he could experience changes in his center of gravity and begin to respond when his balance was threatened. We rolled the beach ball over Ned as he lay on the floor so that he could feel the sensation of pressure. He loved that, and it calmed him. We bought an electric vibrator and stimulated his hands and arms and feet and neck. We rubbed him. We took him to the beach and rubbed sand on him. He was sleeping on terry cloth sheets. It was all fun to do and Ned enjoyed it. And this was a portable therapy. We could take it with us wherever we went.

Pasadena, California
July 26, 1973

Dear Mother:

I have just made our reservations. The boys and I arrive in Hartford next Wednesday at 5:55 P.M.—American Airlines.

Wanted to let you know that Ned is now on a special diet. This is part of the megavitamin therapy. Don't feel you have to stock up or prepare. It isn't that hard. Basically it's high protein, low fat, low carbohydrate. No refined sugars.

Dr. Salley says that we can be fairly casual about it, but I think it is best to be strict at home and more lenient out so that an occasional ice cream cone will be okay. Also so that he can have a trip to McDonald's or Shakey's now and then. The emphasis should be on the protein intake, not on the things he can't have. Occasional goodies are okay. Not only okay but important. Dr. Salley says that the scientific reasons for such a diet are not well documented but that experience has shown that megavitamins are effective only in combination with a high protein diet. We are easing him into it, and the diet may become more strict when we see her in September.

John is allowed goodies, of course, but as he loves yogurt, he can have that. I think it will be better to omit cookies, etc., from the home scene and take John out for treats. I don't want to make it too hard on Ned and besides John isn't used to a lot of sweets.

We are really going to be lots of trouble. Are you sure you want us?

Can Jim rig up a tire swing, as it is great for Ned's occupational therapy?

Back to Watergate. Mitchell seems an awful man. I don't think I believe him.

See you soon. Love, B.

Bill was hard at work on the second season of "M*A*S*H," and I took both boys, their toys, and a bag full of vitamins to Connecticut to visit my mother and Jim. My mother had been in on all that was happening with Ned, and she had visited us enough to know him pretty well. She wasn't apprehensive about his coming into her lovely little house. She cleverly turned the garage into a boys' room. It was so cozy and attractive with a carpet and beds and lots of play space. Ned's half was decorated with flags. We hadn't been there long before Ned had shredded every little paper flag to bits. "I thought he would love them," said his poor grandmother. I guess I had forgotten to tell her how much his tearing had increased. With her usual positive energy, she shrugged it off. She finally had her grandchildren with her, and we were all going to have a wonderful time.

My mother and Jim were willing to take Ned on while I took John to visit friends in New York. John was seven now, and it was time he saw a real city. And it was our city, after all. I wanted John to see where we had lived in Greenwich Village and the theaters Bill had worked in, on Broadway and off.

Glastonbury, Connecticut
August 22, 1973

Dear Bill:

Well, I recovered from my climb to the top of the Statue of Liberty—just barely. It wasn't so bad while it was happening as the temperature inside the S. of L. was about 120 degrees, which makes the muscles very limber, but next day I was very, very stiff.

My mother and Jim were worn out from running after Ned for two days. So we stayed home on Sunday and prepared for camping. (We took a short drive to see a covered bridge—lovely.) Monday we took off for a very nice campground in Rhode Island. We got there around noon and spent the greater part of the day setting up camp. We rented a beautiful tent for Ned, John, and me. Sounds like fun doesn't it? Really not without you. I am hard to please. I like to look at Sequoias and bears and you. Some such combination is necessary for my enjoyment of any but perfect conditions.

Well, on Tuesday we had a nice day swimming in the pond and walking about. John found friends and played baseball. Unfortunately, Jim discovered that the camper wouldn't start and we spent the rest of the day waiting for the mechanic. The news was bad. So instead of going out for a lobster dinner we raced to the camp store, bought a can of beans, and got back in time to see the camper towed away. We all five slept in the tent, which would not have been bad except that a terrific storm came up. Torrential rain and winds. We were lucky not to have to abandon the tent in the night. Many did. Some slept in one foot of water! Ugh! But it was bad enough. This A.M., after absolutely NO sleep, we were rescued by an organization aptly called FISH and driven to Glastonbury. Jim was not rescued and is staying until he can find out what to do about the poor camper.

We were numb when we got home but cleaned boys and selves and clothes (of course, the dryer broke down!) before my mother collapsed and went to bed. I walked over to get the mail and your letter was smiling at me.

I had hoped to go to New York to do grown-up things. (I do love N.Y. It is such fun and so exciting and just the same and different and beautiful and dirty and everything it always has been and I can't wait to go there with Y-O-U.) Anyway, I don't see how I can. I don't think my mother is up to both boys for two days.

Tomorrow I must get my tickets, take care of clothes (laundromat, ugh!), etc. Tomorrow, too, if the camper has not recovered, someone will have to go get Jim and our things. I am going to Goodspeed Opera House with Joan and Roger on Monday night and on Thursday we depart! I will NEVER leave you for such a long time again. Nothing makes sense without you.

Letter interrupted by a tearing episode. Can't wait till Chicago.

Many kisses, B.

Glastonbury, Connecticut
August 22, 1973

Dear Daddy from John,
The boys' room is very nice. We have gone camping. I hope that you have a good time. I hope you do not lose my quartz crystal. I miss you. We are home but Jim is still at the camp because the camper has lost the power for the battery.

I've found some more rocks. I have found a rock that is just like my gold one. I have taken my gold rock on the trip. We have gone to New York. New York is very crowded.

Love, John

PS I'll see you in Chicago, Ill., at your father's house.

There was a little piece of paper enclosed with John's letter. In a spidery hand and large letters it said, "Love, Ned."

CHAPTER 4

Special

I waited eagerly at the gate at O'Hare Airport for a glimpse of Barbara and the boys. I had thought of them often while I worked at the studio, wondering what they were up to. On my days off I had kept myself busy puttering around in the garden and painting an old glass-fronted bookcase to house John's rapidly expanding rock collection. My little family and I had never been apart for more than a few days, and the month's separation had seemed endless. John, his usual robust self, came running toward me. Barbara followed, holding Ned by the hand. I greeted them with hugs and kisses, but when I lifted Neddie up, holding him close, I was somehow unprepared for the gentle stream of noises I encountered. "My," I thought to myself, "he buzzes just like a little motor. Odd I should have forgotten that." From the moment we brought Ned home, he had been surrounded by a cloud of self-generated sound. First he was a restless sleeper, then a crib rocker; and then he developed a pattern of continual vocalizations that sometimes formed themselves into language. Ned did not appear to realize that he made these sounds. When he had something to say, or when he was paying very close attention to something being said to him, or when he was concentrating mightily on a task like balancing one block on top of another, they stopped, but not for long.

We piled into the car and drove off to my parents' home in Glencoe, the house I grew up in and which had been in my family since it was built in 1900. I had been looking forward to this day, to being at the old house, to spending time together, all of us, the boys and Barbara and my parents. Living on the West Coast meant that we didn't have these chances often, and I felt it was important that my mother and father see something of the boys as they grew up. I also wanted my boys to have the fun of knowing their grandparents and knowing the peaceful suburb that I looked back on so fondly. However, I could see that Barbara was ready to be back in Pasadena, ready to resume our usual life. A whole month with the boys in surroundings unfamiliar to them hadn't been easy.

My brother Tom and his wife lived a few blocks away from my parents. They had a twenty-month-old baby, and Ned at five towered over him. Ned was interested in Gregory, but his approach was not gentle enough. "What's the matter with you?" said my father crossly. "Don't you know you have to be careful with babies?" Ned was abashed. He left Gregory alone, completely alone. He retreated into his own world of blocks and flags. I couldn't bring myself to explain how we were coming to view Ned. The word "handicapped" didn't come easily to me. I knew Ned took a lot of special understanding and special handling if he were going to behave in an acceptable way. His approach to other children was such a tenuous thing; it really should be nurtured and there were so few opportunities to do so. But a four-day visit was not going to allow time for teaching him how to play with his little cousin or for instructing other family members in the subtleties that helped so much with Ned. Speaking to him calmly and gently was always more effective. But I didn't think my dad would see eye-to-eye with that point of view. After all, booming out orders had worked for him in raising three sons, and we had all turned out just fine. Tom and Judy quite naturally felt protective of their little boy. Who could blame them? Perhaps the next time we got together things would be better. Ned might have made a lot of progress by then.

A few days later we were back home in Pasadena, and school was beginning. True, we had not met our goal of regular kindergarten by age five, but at least Ned had been admitted into the aphasic kindergarten of the Pasadena public school system. Perhaps with the language help he would get in a class where the teacher was a speech therapist, he would make the expected strides. The class was located in a regular school, and he would have plenty of exposure to normal kids on the playground and in the lunchroom; that just had to be good for Ned. School started with all the usual excitement. New clothes and a new lunchbox and new hopes.

Pasadena, California
September 12, 1973

Dear Mother:

We have been as busy as possible since our visit to Glencoe but we are settling in at last. School began last week and is going exactly as expected for John. He is in a mixed (first, second, and third grades) class.

Ned is easing into his program. His teacher is young and has a lovely manner. Unfortunately the school has not yet hired an aide for her so she is too busy. She has asked that Ned only go a half day for the time being until an aide is hired. So I have been driving over to pick him up and having lunch with the kids. There are six of them. Ned's communication problem is right in the middle but there is no denying that he is more difficult and requires more individual attention than the others. I have offered to help but am trying not to come on too strong. I am more nervous about this than I had realized. It means so much to have him in school and making the expected progress. I won't be too upset if he doesn't make it but I will be upset if I feel that he wasn't really given a chance. I sound pessimistic, which I really am not—nervous, yes! I'll know more soon.

The school is very regimented. For example: the children— normal, regular classrooms as well as the three handicapped classes—walk in lines to lunch. The principal stands up in the lunchroom and yells at misbehaviors through a P.A. system. Kids must eat quickly—ten minutes—and raise their hands for permission to leave the lunchroom! None of this will hurt Ned, but it gives an idea of a very inflexible administration.

Bill is working this week and last and we go to the "M*A*S*H" opening night party on Saturday. Love to Jim. We miss you both.

Love, B.

It didn't start quite as we had hoped. Not only was Ned not welcome for a complete school day but until the aide arrived, the teacher wanted help from Barbara in the classroom. Spending time there opened her eyes to what was considered adequate for aphasic children by our school district. School had begun in a classroom without suitable materials. There were four or five puzzles, all with many, many pieces—far too advanced for kindergarten-age children, even normal ones. And that was it! As to the playground, the special children were not expected to mix with the normal kids. They had their own playground. But the deep trenches beneath the swings made them too high for even agile Ned to climb up on. The ground was covered with bits of trash, broken glass, and horse droppings, for the school was located in a horsey area and on weekends the neighbors rode there. I was furious. This was just not going to do. I was on the phone to the superintendent's office, and I got a modicum of cooperation from the school district. I went over to the school with the assistant superintendent and pointed out the problems. The playground was cleaned up and the fence was locked on weekends. The swings were lowered. Slowly, supplies and materials trickled into the classroom. The aide also arrived.

Then another problem surfaced. The special bus that picked Ned up at the door wasn't working out. He had begun to disrobe during the ride and to throw his clothes out the window. "I think he's trying to tell us something," said Dr. Salley when we called to ask her what to do. For the time being, until he was more comfortable with the routine, we would drive him to school as well as pick him up. Well, that would be okay. We would do anything to make this work for Ned.

We didn't know what other choices we might have, but the news from the aphasic kindergarten was not good, and each day was getting a little more tense.

Dear Mr. and Mrs. Christopher: Ned threw Danny's lunchbox out and broke it. He (Danny) was very upset over this as it was his only one.

Dear Mr. and Mrs. Christopher: Our new math and reading programs are lasting longer than originally anticipated. Could Ned come at 10:55?

This meant that Barbara had to drop Ned off at 10:55 and pick him up at noon, not much of a school day.

Ned does not get a flag today as he threw Elsie's lunchbox at recess. I think it would be good if Mrs. Christopher came on Thursdays and Fridays as I do not yet have a volunteer.

We had a reevaluation meeting with Dr. Salley, and we first discussed the things that were going well for Ned. He was beginning to smile when people greeted him. He had learned to observe his sidewalk boundaries in front of our house and was no longer wandering into the street. He could now stand on one foot, then the other, in dressing. He could swing on the overhead ladder and perform other goal-directed activities. He was more graceful and relaxed. He would catch himself when falling. He was riding his trike with vigor and interest, coasting and pushing with one foot. He had become very interested in looking at himself in the mirror. He still liked to stare at his fingers but was doing that much less. He was able to listen when upset. His diction was improved. The hair pulling had magically disappeared. And sometimes he watched TV. (He loved the "M*A*S*H" helicopters but was relatively indifferent to my appearance.) We told Dr. Salley how pleased we were with his occupational therapy and that we attributed the progress he had made to sensory integration.

Then we discussed the problems—the throwing, the tearing, the floods of "jargon" (which is what his continual verbal noises were now being called), the times of physical tension and confusion. The school psychologist had told us that she was wondering whether Ned belonged in the aphasic kindergarten. She questioned Ned's ability to learn, and she was especially concerned about his effect on the other children. We wondered if we were doing the right thing in continuing to work so hard to keep him in a school program that seemed to be going nowhere and where he seemed so unwelcome.

Dr. Salley suggested that we not pull Ned out of the aphasic kindergarten just yet. But she thought we had better do the groundwork for getting Ned into private school, the Dubnoff School if possible. Meanwhile she suggested that Ned attend the normal kindergarten class for part of his day to see how that would go. The principal reluctantly allowed it, but only if Barbara or an aide could accompany him. Perhaps Ned could play on the playground with the normal children? Well, yes. But he was merely tolerated. When my shooting schedule allowed, I went over to the school. I thought Ned was doing pretty well on the playground. He would wait in line for a turn on the swings, and he could swing and climb as well as any kid. But the aides assigned to the playground complained that he stayed on the swing too long. "Get that little disaster out of here!" They clearly felt that Ned's teacher should keep her children separate.

> Dear Mr. and Mrs. Christopher: Ned earned a flag today. He went to the kindergarten room today and played with the big blocks.

> Ned did not earn his flag today as he threw his flags. In the auditorium he makes too much noise and sets a poor example for the other special-ed classes. He went to kindergarten today and listened at the listening center.

> Ned earned a flag today. He sewed a stocking today and went to the discovery room.

> Will Ned come with someone tomorrow and Friday? He had trouble at lunch today as he threw his yogurt.

There were ups and downs but by Christmas vacation it was clear that Ned would not be able to continue in the aphasic kindergarten. Fortunately, we had followed Dr. Salley's advice and had started the application process at Dubnoff.

We had heard of the Dubnoff School. At the Fisher Clinic we

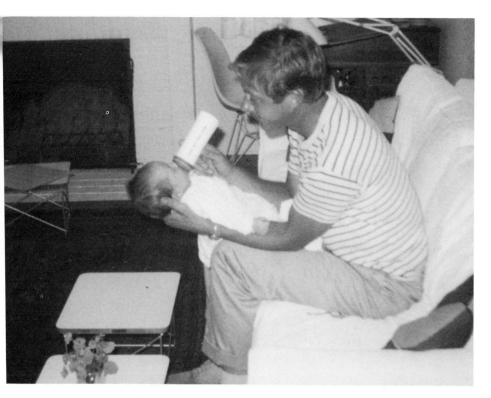

(Above) Bill feeding infant Ned, who has "stiffened himself into a board." 1968.

(Right) Ned on his first birthday. In the garden, Studio City. May 1969.

(Above) The William Christopher family visiting Bill's parents. Ned is "stimming" on his fingers. Christmas 1969.

(Above right) Two-year-old Ned standing in the vegetable garden that provided his first words. Summer 1970.

(Below right) Ned and his flag cake. Third birthday, May 1971.

(Left) Father Mulcahy and his son Ned. Spring 1975.

(Above) "Laughing Cloud," "Talking Sky," and Ned in the garden. Pasadena, 1973.

(Right) Three-year-old Ned starting one of his "layouts." May 1971.

(Above) Harry and the boys. 1976.

(Left) Ned saying good-bye to Robin at the end of the school day. 1976.

(Above right) Ned and John on a family hike. 1976.

(Below right) "I am eating some broccoli and some chicken," wrote Ned's speech therapist under this teaching photo. 1977.

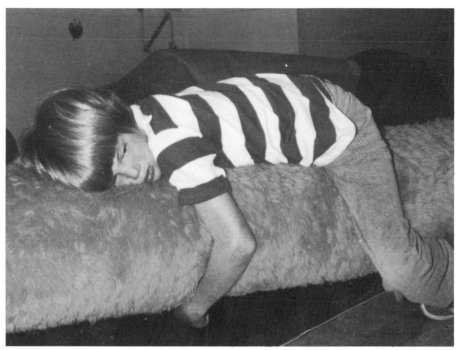

(Above) Ned hugging the "horse" in an occupational therapy session. 1977.

(Below) Looking at flags, one of Ned's favorite activities. 1977.

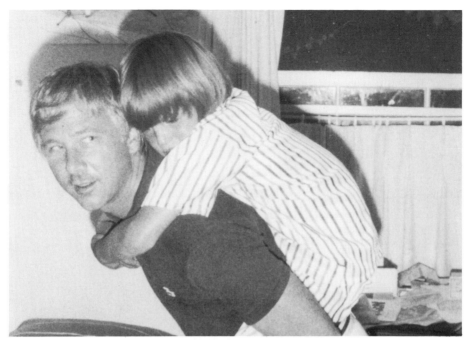

(Above) Ned finally did come to like piggyback. 1977.

(Below) Ned taking his Ritalin. May 1977.

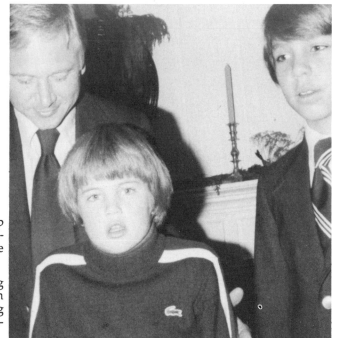

(Right) All dressed up and going out to dinner. New Year's Eve 1977.

(Below) "I am mixing the pancakes." "I am stirring with a big spoon." Another teaching photo, 1977.

(Above) Ned making a silly face. With Margarita, 1977.

(Below) Ned shielding his ear from the sound as he puts a record on the phonograph. 1977.

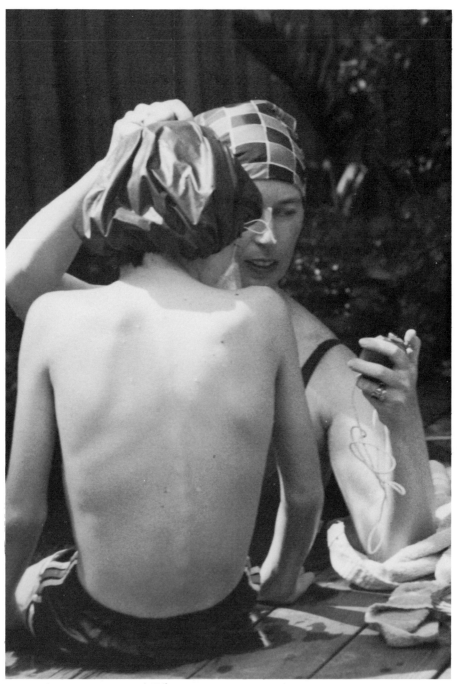

(Above) Getting started on Ned's first Institutes program, Barbara uses a stopwatch to time a one-minute masking. 1978.

had talked to other parents who were trying to get their kids into Dubnoff. At that time, we had been planning on regular kindergarten, or at worst a special kindergarten for a short time. We had wanted Ned to be with normal kids; we hadn't considered the possibility of another school with all handicapped kids. But our point of view was changing. Dubnoff was run by full-fledged professionals who had been helping kids for a long time. They provided a program that would not require one of us to be there every minute. Perhaps if we could get Ned into Dubnoff, Barbara and I could resume a more normal life, even if Ned's schooling did have to be special education. But what if they wouldn't take him? What if all the places were filled?

Barbara had been reading about how children acquire language, and she worked out a program of her own to try to help Ned until we had him settled in school. Meanwhile we threw ourselves on Mrs. Jordan's mercy.

Pasadena, California
January 11, 1974

Dear Mother:

Just a hasty note. I am really swamped these days as Ned has returned to Mrs. Jordan's nursery school, and they would only take him if I would work there as a mother-helper. (Two and a half hours each afternoon.) I have started my own regular morning "education" sessions with Ned, am working one morning a week at John's school, and have jury duty every other Thursday. Bill has been working every week on "M*A*S*H." So I am very busy. However, we have begun our interviews at Dubnoff, one this week, three next week, and with luck, they will accept Ned for a February class. If so, he will be in school from nine to two daily! Keep your fingers crossed! If this doesn't work out I don't know what we can do.

If you are snowed in and have nothing to do (?) you could help my new language program for Ned by clipping magazine pictures. What I need are good, clear pictures of objects and of people doing things. Photographs are best as drawings can be confusing. Right now I am also looking for pictures that show emotional reactions—sad, happy, mad, etc.—and pictures that illustrate use of the senses. Tasting, smelling, listening, looking—these are hard to find. Also categories: animals, furniture, clothing, vehicles, toys, etc. You would be thrilled by his progress. Yesterday he answered the phone for me when I was busy and carried on a conversation. Luckily the caller was Bill! He is doing well in nursery school and joins in group activities pretty well. Much, much more spontaneous language, face more expressive.

Problems—still doesn't initiate social contact with anyone except family, and the eternal noises, tearing, and throwing. However, as communication improves, I feel optimistic about everything. I'm sure that my teaching him is helping greatly. He reminds me that it's "time to do our work."

Well—Ned and I have to have lunch before we leave for nursery school. Some good soup for a cold day. 40s and 50s here.

Love and kisses to you both, B.

On the days when Barbara worked in John's classroom, she took Ned along, and that was going remarkably well. "Is he deaf or retarded?" asked one of the second-graders in a matter-of-fact voice. There were special education classes in John's school, and the kids there were integrated into the normal classrooms as much as possible. This second-grader recognized Ned as a "special-ed kid" with total acceptance.

John's teacher included Ned in the class activities, and she happened just then to be teaching her class about flags! Here at least Ned could show off; even a special-ed kid could do that if given a chance. He colored the flag outlines, sitting very appropriately alongside the normal children.

The children in the class were writing "books." They would write little stories, and Barbara and the other mothers would bind them. So Ned wrote a book too, just like the other kids. He dictated his story to Barbara: "Once upon a time I had a California flag. And I put it up, up, up on the palm tree. And I put it up, up, up on the house. And I put it up, up, up in the flag holder. Then I took it down. And I put it with my stop sign. Then I went night-night. And I put it on my bed. Good-night,

Flag. The End." Of course, he needed a lot of prompting to get him through the story. Barbara bound the little book, and Ned was an author!

Coloring flags in John's class gave Ned a good idea. Getting up early one morning, he found some drawing pens and created big flag murals on the dining room walls. They were colored correctly. They were beautiful. "Japanese!" "Italian!" "Irish!"

Since the public schools had a responsibility to educate Ned, and since they had been unable to find a suitable classroom for him, they sent a home teacher. She called first on the telephone: "Yes, I think I know how to approach Ned. I have read his record. He is a slow learner." As Barbara hung up the phone, she said with a sigh, "I don't think he's a slow learner at all." Well, we would wait and see what the home teacher thought when she met Ned. Fortunately, she didn't think he was a slow learner for long. As soon as she met him, she was impressed with his intelligence, and she brought loads of materials with her every afternoon. Ned worked in math and reading workbooks; he built structures with little blocks according to diagrams she provided; he practiced making the letters of the alphabet. Miss Schenden took him for walks and did what she could to elicit language. He liked Miss Schenden and she liked him. As always, it was comforting to deal with someone who saw Ned as bright. We began to see that this was one of the clues to dealing with him. When teachers or therapists considered him retarded and treated him as such, he didn't do well. When they recognized that he was bright and gave him challenging material to work with, he could do very well. Or pretty well. Or well enough to give us hope.

Finally, we got the happy news. Ned had been accepted by the Dubnoff School, one of the most reputable special education schools in the Los Angeles area. Their philosophy was that of providing individualized help for a wide variety of problems in the most normal setting possible. There were class outings, a swimming pool, a beautiful playground. There were other Dubnoff kids who lived in Pasadena, so we could car-pool for the fourteen-mile drive. Ned was assigned to a very experienced teacher. Betty Fried plunged him into work and play in her small and colorful classroom. It was wonderful to have him settled in school, but as the initial elation wore off, Barbara and I began to feel nervous again. After the disaster of his aphasic kindergarten, we were afraid to count on anything. We couldn't help being aware that Ned's problems seemed greater than those of the other Dubnoff kids; most of them had what struck us as rather mild learning disabilities.

"They usually don't take autistic kids here," one of the other parents said.

"Well, Ned's doctor doesn't consider him autistic."

We had our fingers crossed that Dubnoff was the right track we had been searching for so long.

By the time spring came on, life had fallen into a regular routine. We car-pooled to Dubnoff. Twice a week we took Ned to see Mary for occupational therapy. He had his megavitamins and his special diet. We had the benefit of Dr. Salley's regular consultations. Ned was happy, and life at home was certainly more normal.

Pasadena, California
April 8, 1974

Dear Mother and Jim:

I am so tired I will probably fall asleep while writing! We are cleaning out the garage. This job hasn't been done since Jim and Bill did it over two years ago! We were inspired by our recent purchase of a new washing machine and dryer. Well, we couldn't put those lovely, new, expensive machines in that messy garage. So we have been slaving! Bill is building shelves everywhere! I'm even washing the Clorox bottles. We are quite carried away with ourselves but eventually will have an organized: workshop, silk-screen shop, gardening area, laundry. With luck we will also be able to get in a car or two.

We are also very busy in the yard. We had some tree work done—surgery and pruning on the avocado tree, pruning two big eucalyptus, removal of five dead or dying trees. Now everything looks bare but better and we are planting like crazy. Vegetables too!

All this frantic work effort must be completed by the end of the *month when "M*A*S*H" resumes, at which point Bill will completely lose interest.*

The boys are on vacation this week, and the weather is great. We went to the beach yesterday.

John is "into" baseball. He is playing on a Little League tee-ball team (right field), watching baseball on TV, clipping the newspaper, talking baseball continually. Today was the "greatest day of his life" because he was watching as Hank Aaron hit #715, or was it #315?

Thank you for the Easter check for clothes for the boys. You are generous and they will be very well dressed. I haven't bought their outfits yet but will get John into Bullock's this week. He is supposed to write you to thank you for the $10 but it's so hard to write with a baseball mitt on (which is what he bought with the "something for yourself" part of the money).

Ned is making progress but somehow I am hoping to see something more from him. Even though his language, behavior, abilities all move forward, it just isn't coming together. Perhaps I am simply becoming more objective as he is away from home for six hours a day. Perhaps it is that as he grows older, the gap between Ned and a normal child becomes more obvious. He will be six next month and is so far from what John was at that age. We see Dr. Salley at the end of next week, and she always makes me feel better.

I am falling asleep. Happy Easter.

Love, Barbara

PS Here is a drawing of Ned's for your refrigerator.

Dr. Salley had a new idea for us. A research geneticist was investigating a possible link between Ned's kind of problem and diseases such as Huntington's chorea. He wanted to meet Ned, and one day before my shooting schedule took over my life, I drove Ned to his office. The doctor took tissue samples from Ned's leg to study, something to do with the blood platelets. He didn't promise that he would find anything helpful in the short run, but perhaps the future would hold an answer for Ned and all the kids like him. Meanwhile, he suggested that Ned might be having mini-seizures, possibly as many as a thousand per day. This was an interesting idea. It meant that Ned's perceptions would be like those of a person in and out of a dream. The thousand moments in each day when he was not taking in information might be the reason his language had not developed properly. It might explain why his sensory experiences were not normal. It might explain everything. Dr. Salley thought that small doses of medication to inhibit seizures would be worth a try. Ned was put on Orexin, and it had an immediate positive result. Another anticonvulsant, Zarontin, was added. Ned continued to improve.

Dubnoff cautiously said that Ned would be accepted for summer school, although we would have to wait and see about the fall. Things were looking up. We felt good enough about everything to leave the children while we spent two days with old friends who were visiting from New York.

Pasadena, California
June 17, 1974

Dear Mother and Jim:

Just a quick note, which I will try to get into the mail at once. We had a great weekend in San Francisco with Joan and Roger. We shopped and talked and walked and went to the tops of about six tall buildings. Much eating and drinking. (+ 3 lbs.!) Bought a darling jacket with Joan's encouragement and your money. Thank you!

Harry did a good job with the children—took them to the zoo and the beach and of course Shakey's and McDonald's. Every morning the first thing Ned says when he sees us is, "Where's Harry?"

Ned is doing quite well, we think. His new medicine is having a very good effect on him. He is much calmer and much more tuned in.

John is out of school now. He will go to day camp in August. Ned finishes up on Friday and we leave for a two-week vacation at Balboa Island on Saturday. Bill will be shooting the first week and I have one day of jury duty the second, but still it will be good to be away.

Garden is going great! How is yours?

L. & K., B.

We didn't have any relatives in California but we did have Harry, the same Harry who had taken care of our house when we went to Canada, a college friend of Barbara's who had assigned himself as a favorite uncle to our children. Ned adored him. Ned's friendships were always clearly made. He either liked people right away or they didn't seem to exist for him.

Some places, too, attracted Ned right away. Balboa Island was one.

Balboa Island, California
July 6, 1974

Dear Mother and Jim:

Tomorrow is our last day here and we are very sorry to leave. The boys are brown and I am fat but we are all happy. Ned has learned to play in the sand and swim in the sea. John has been enjoying himself by going to the little beach (without us) and shopping (without us) and out for ice cream (without us). I think you would like Balboa Island. Very small and fun—cute restaurants and shops, a promenade around the edge, many boats. We can take a ferry to a "Fun Zone" with ferris wheel, etc., and to the big ocean beach. We have had perfect weather and have missed miserable heat at home.

L. & K., B.

The delights of Balboa ushered in official summer. And in summer the shooting for the fall television season was in full swing. I was spending most of my days working at the studio or on the set in the Malibu hills, a location chosen for its resemblance to the landscape of Korea. John was spending hours in the garage with his cronies making model boats out of scrap lumber. The gang would troop down into the Arroyo Seco to sail them in the casting pond. Then back to the garage for alterations and back again to the Arroyo. We offered a penny bounty on snails, and the gang scoured the back yard filling coffee cans with slimy creatures. We took picnics to the beach in the late afternoons and watched the sun go down into the Pacific while the heat of the day dispersed into the sky over Pasadena.

Summer introduced Ned to someone else whom he loved on sight, Robin Wynslow. She was to be his new teacher in the fall. Robin had a theater background, and we liked that. Theater people know how to work, and they tend to be flexible, and, in the words of the old song, they're the best people I know. She had taught normal kids for six years, and we liked that too. Many people in special education didn't seem to know much about normal kids. How could they help Ned become more normal if they didn't understand normalcy? And she was pretty. By this time we were well aware how important that was for Ned.

Pasadena, California
August 30, 1974

Dear Mother and Jim:

Your letter reminded me that I have been most remiss in my correspondence.

This is Ned's last week of summer school. It has been very successful. Ned has improved his swimming and has done well with his schoolwork. Behavior is remarkably improved. It is definite that he will be continuing at Dubnoff. All concerned are very pleased with his progress: Dubnoff staff, Dr. Salley, and us. Of course, having Ned's immediate future settled is very important to our peace of mind.

Bill is back to work on "M*A*S*H" this week in a script that features Father Mulcahy.

We ran into Inga Swenson at the Hollywood Bowl last week. I haven't seen her for years and years. She is going to be staying on the West Coast and Lowell and their younger son will be following her soon. Inga came here for dinner, and Ned was in the bathtub when she arrived. He heard her voice and curiosity got

*the better of him. He climbed out of the tub and peeked through
the door. One glimpse of her and he ran dripping and naked into
the living room and leapt into her arms. Inga said she had never
had such a greeting and I can believe it. I am so happy to have
reestablished contact with her. She is even more beautiful now,
and a lovely person.*

*John has had a fine summer. He loved camp. He went three
days a week for four weeks and has also enjoyed the neighborhood
gang thoroughly. Today he is at a birthday party in the afternoon
and a Dodger ball game tonight. Being his social secretary is
among my heaviest responsibilities.*

*Garden notes: Our vegetables were terrific until about two
weeks ago, when plants started dying.*

*We are planning to go to Sequoia for two days, weekend after
this one. Then school begins!*

Love to you both, Barbara

In the classroom Robin was demanding and energetic. Each
child had his own program for academics, but there were plenty
of group activities too. Each day was carefully structured, and
Ned progressed nicely. He worked each morning on reading
and language. In the afternoons he worked in a math workbook,
practiced writing, painted pictures. The expectations were
enough of a challenge to keep Ned on his toes, but not beyond
his capabilities. Robin knew that she couldn't lower her
demands on Ned without losing his interest.

Of course, Robin was stymied by some of Ned's behaviors,
one of which had been driving us crazy for some time now: leaf
tearing. We had been able to persuade him to leave the house
plants alone, but anything growing outdoors he considered
fair game, and if allowed to do so, he would spend hours
tearing leaves into tiny pieces. One day in September Barbara
drove to Dubnoff to pick up Ned. She and Robin and Julie,
another of the teachers, sat on the lawn talking while Ned ran
about in the background, stopping frequently to tear leaves.
They chatted away, discussing possible reasons and remedies
for leaf tearing until suddenly Robin burst out laughing. "Just
look at what we're all doing!" she said looking down.

In front of each of them was a little mound of shredded blades of grass.

There were days when Ned was still lost in his own world, unable or unwilling to join in group activities, but he consistently brought home completed worksheets and samples of his writing to show that quite a lot was happening in school. And swimming and bowling and outings were usually quite successful.

Pasadena, California
November 21, 1974

Dear Mother:

Everything is fine. You wouldn't be able to tell from my long silence, but that is due to our very busy schedule and not to low spirits.

Ned is off tomorrow on his first "overnight." His teacher, Robin, is taking all seven children to her house near the beach. "Camping out" on her living room floor. Many exciting activities planned. It really is a milestone. He is doing well in school and, Robin reports, is much more spontaneous in his talking, much more able to focus on his work. We think his new medicine is contributing to this. We see Dr. Salley on Monday.

"M*A*S*H" is through for the season. Hope you saw the one two weeks ago where Bill did a sermon! Written by Jim Fritzell and Everett Greenbaum.

You'll never believe and I blush to admit that I now have a cleaning lady. One day every other week. What a fantastic luxury, and it has really given me a lift.

Love and kisses to you both, B.

At this point Margarita entered our lives. Though it took some getting used to, we were really delighted to have some household help. As it turned out, Margarita was much more than that. She was another conquest for Ned. She loved him unreservedly. And he loved her. From that time on anyone who did a lick of work around the house was called Margarita. My parents visited us that year and my mother, pitching in to help us get the house ready for a photographic interview, was on her hands and knees under the piano cleaning the floor when Ned came home from school. "Margarita!" he greeted her. My mother understood that this was a high compliment.

Ned was now taking a third anticonvulsant, Mysoline. At first it seemed to help his cognitive abilities and keep him calm and focused, but that was only for a few weeks. We went, as had become our tradition, to Bob and Leona's for Thanksgiving. ("Over the river and through the woods to Leona's house we go," we would sing on the freeway.) At dinner Ned had a very strange episode. He began flinging the dinner plates about the room. We were appalled. There was turkey and potato all over the floor, broken china, Ned at the kids' table getting wilder every second. Barbara and I rushed over and tried to calm him, but he was unreachable. We took him out of the room and off to a bedroom where Barbara and Leona did their best to soothe him. The tension in his small body was fierce. I stood in the doorway numbly as they tried to get Ned to lie down on the bed. I felt helpless, but I could see they were having the right effect. Barbara was crying as she rubbed him. Ned had never done anything like this before. He had broken a flower pot or two and had fiddled with some light fixtures, but this was a new level of excitability and destructiveness. Leona and Bob helped us clean up the mess, and eventually Ned calmed down. "Perhaps," suggested Leona, "he's jealous of the baby." (Her new nephew was among the guests.) "Or, maybe he's just overstimulated from all the people and all the food." It seemed that as soon as things would begin to go well for Ned, something would happen and all our worries would return.

Dr. Salley canceled the Mysoline. There was immediate improvement but Ned's leaf tearing and throwing increased, and Robin noted that his fine-motor work showed some deterioration. It was months before we felt that he had completely recovered, but there were no further wild episodes.

Pasadena, California
January 13, 1975

Dear Mother:
Everyone is back on schedule after the holidays. We did have a lovely Christmas this year, and the bonus of excellent weather for

the whole two-week vacation. The good weather continues: no smog, clear, bright, spring-like days, but we do need rain very badly and so I feel guilty wishing this could go on and on.

Your Christmas presents for the boys are very successful. John loves his radio and the football suit. I love the toy McDonald's for Ned. He is beginning to play with it now. He certainly recognizes it and understands it. I think it was a perfect choice for him. I bought some books and a record for Ned. He is quite interested in reading, as he calls it. One of his favorite activities is to get out a lot of books at once and go through them.

On New Year's Day we had a large group (forty) for the parade, including Ned's classmates and their families. It was great fun and seemed quite effortless. I think it's having Ned in a good school that has me feeling better than I have in years.

Now it's time to stop eating and drinking and get busy around our house and garden.

Time to go pick Ned up at school.

Love and kisses, B.

Nineteen seventy-five was gliding smoothly by, and we were getting pretty relaxed about a lot of things. Ned wasn't becoming normal, but he was holding his own. We were happy about his school, and the following summer we went back to Balboa Island for a vacation. We knew that being involved in as many normal family activities as possible was something we had to keep doing for Ned, for John, and for ourselves.

Pasadena, California
July 14, 1975

Dear Mother:

Our Balboa vacation was marvelous. Ned has improved so much that I was able to let him go to the little beach alone with John. (One day he made 100 sand cakes!) I could stay at the house or run to the market without worrying.

Bill was quite busy during those two weeks. He has shot the first "M*A*S*H" of the season and has signed a five-year contract. (This means, of course, five years only if "M*A*S*H" lasts that long.)

Ned is in summer school. He goes from nine to six and is thriving on it, and I hardly need to say what a break it is for me to have so much free time. John is home, of course, but so busy with baseball and friends that he only checks in for occasional contact with home (perhaps I should call it home plate).

We all send LOVE and are thinking of you. Especially me!

Love, Barbara

In October Dr. Salley requested a consultation with a neurologist, so we were off for a new battery of tests. Dr. Evans didn't find anything neurologically wrong with Ned. His EEG was normal, and there was no reason to have him on any anticonvulsants. Dr. Evans did think that Ritalin, a stimulant that works in reverse on many hyperactive children, might help Ned. He had attention span problems; he could be called hyperactive. We decided to try it. Again, Ned seemed to do well—very well, in fact.

Dr. Evans also said it was possible that Ned was subject to allergies and that a diet free of cow's milk might help. He was allowed goat's milk, and we sent a thermos of goat's milk and homemade goat's milk yogurt to Dubnoff with him every day. That was a nuisance but only occasionally a problem.

Dear Robin:
It's mating season for goats.

Barbara

Ned was enjoying his second year in Robin's class. Things were going so well that we were beginning to forget all the ups and downs of the previous year. Thanksgiving at Bob and Leona's (it's wonderful to have friends who don't give up!) went very smoothly. Ritalin and the diet were helping, and maybe Ned was beginning to catch up to himself. His long period of good behavior made us feel that we could do something we had been thinking about for some time. We would give John a puppy for Christmas. John had wanted a dog, but we had been afraid that Ned would be too rough on a pet. What's more, he had been terrified of dogs since he was knocked down by a boisterous retriever in Stanley Park in Vancouver years ago. Now that Ned was seven and a half and so much easier, we thought it would work out, if we chose carefully and found a sturdy, loving little puppy. We picked Pepper out of a litter of beagles. From the first he had an easygoing disposition. We had read that beagles make very good pets but that they must be treated very gently when puppies. We emphasized this to John, and he took it so much to heart that he sat quietly in the beanbag chair in the boys' room holding the puppy in his arms for the entire first week of Pepper's residence in our family. Pepper settled in completely, and it soon became clear that if he were going to be happy, he would have to live in the boys' room. I took off the closet door and made a place for him right there. Of course when summer came and he was older, he would be moving outside to a dog house, an arrangement we thought only proper; but we wouldn't tell Pepper about that just yet. Ned was wonderful with the dog; he wasn't afraid of him at all. Another piece in our picture of normal family life was in place.

Ned was unusually healthy. He hardly ever got sick. And so was John—most of the time:

Pasadena, California
January 22, 1976

Dear Grandma and Grandpa:

Well first of all how is the wether back in the East? Bad news, for the last copel of days I have been sick. I have the flue and it's been cinde of dull around here. I don't feel very well. I was going to wright this letter in cursive but I don't feel well enough. Don't worry my next letter will be in cursive.

Love, John

Dear Mother and Jim: I thought I had better send along the enclosed. There has been a complete recovery—handwriting and

(I trust) spelling too! The former patient is now engaged in a report on the San Fernando Mission and will not have time to write or "wright" again soon.

Love, B.

Barbara was finding more time to devote to her art. She had made serigraphs for me to give to my friends on the show at Christmas, and now she had a commission to design and produce a serigraph in an edition of two hundred. We spent every spare minute in the garage silk-screen shop, and Harry helped us run the prints. Soon Barbara was talking about a trip to England with the proceeds. "I want to do something wonderful with this money," she said, "otherwise we'll just spend it all on mustard and laundry soap." So we bought the tickets to England, four of them. We were to visit all of the places Jane Austen had written about in her novels, and all of the places she had visited in her own lifetime. It was to be a pilgrimage of sorts. Barbara had been a "Janeite" for many years, and we had spent vacations reading the novels and letters aloud to each other. We wanted John to go with us. We thought it was about time that he had more exposure to the kinds of things we felt excited about. It was all very well to get excited about the Dodgers; we could do that too, but there were other things in life. As Jane Austen herself had said, "It is well to have as many holds upon happiness as possible." And now that Ned was on Ritalin and was so much more manageable, he would enjoy the trip too. We asked Robin, who had been educated in England, what she thought about our taking Ned along. "The English are very accepting. They have a kind of live-and-let-live attitude," she told us. She didn't think they would pay much attention to our young autistic son.

By this time we weren't fussy about what anyone labeled Ned. Robin called him autistic. In fact, she was going to dedicate her doctoral dissertation on autism to Ned. What does it matter what he's called, as long as he has the right program, we thought, and as long as he is doing well.

So all of us went to England. Harry drove us to the airport; he would take care of the house and garden and Pepper. Ned entertained himself on the plane by making designs on the windows with Colorforms, shapes made out of brilliantly colored thin plastic, some transparent, which would adhere to a window or any smooth surface and which would come off easily without leaving a mark. Actually, he and I walked most of the way over the pole, up and down the aisle. He looked out of the window at the smooth gray ocean below. "It's going!" he said.

The whirlwind of London was something of a shock for Ned. He held both hands over his ears and stared at the traffic. But after a day or two he adjusted. He carried his British flag everywhere, winning hearts with his rosy cheeks—everywhere taken for a native.

"Anyone can see you're British, young man," someone said to him as we stood in line to see the crown jewels.

"Not really; I'm afraid he's American," I said, smiling.

Ned, as usual, didn't speak to strangers. He chased the pigeons in the parks and demonstrated a new skill, standing on his head. He marched willingly along with us wherever we went.

Canterbury
April 18, 1976

Dear Mother:

Yesterday en route here we stopped to visit Godmersham Park, an estate formerly belonging to Jane Austen's brother. I was met at the door by a butler! Mrs. Tritton, the present owner, showed me around the main floor of the house, the drawing room, and gave me sherry in the library. Bill and the boys had drinks outside with Mrs. Tritton's manager. I saw Jane Austen first editions and other valuable J. A. books, a portrait, and some silhouettes of the time of her brother's residence. The estate is now reduced to a mere 2,000 acres. We had hours alone to explore the grounds, now covered with daffodils—the fields full of wild primroses and baby lambs. An amazing and wonderful day.

As to us. Ned is great. He loves traveling. His behavior is very good. The restaurants, hotels, museums, parks all attract him and he is at his best. I think he enjoys all the attention he gets when we are free of our regular duties. All of the above applies to John too, as you would expect—and of course he understands so much and is

*learning so much that it is a great pleasure for us. The plane trip
was simplicity itself.*

*We are enjoying the countryside very much. Traveling here
reminds me of New England when I was growing up. Narrow
roads, small towns, a slower pace. You would love it. We're so
glad we have the children with us. It wouldn't be the same
without them.* •

Much love, B.

We spent three weeks touring Jane Austen's England, and
Ned decorated every hotel window with his Colorforms. He
had transferred his love of design to the vertical plane. The
boys romped in the parks together, Ned reveling in John's
games. Wherever John led, he followed. John's tenth birthday
fell while we were in London and to celebrate the occasion he
wanted to see a cricket match at Lord's. That was fine with
Ned. Four hours of a game none of us understood, perfectly
okay. In our orderly and old-fashioned English hotel, breakfast
was a great experience. The dining room was large, and there
were tables with white linen and jars of honey, ginger
marmalade, preserves, ready and waiting for us every
morning. (It soon became obvious that the sugar-free diet and
the goat's milk were out the window for the duration of the
trip.) The boys would run ahead, John shepherding Ned to the
table. They would eat heartily, toast with lots of honey and
juice and eggs and bacon. Then with the signal, "Come on,
Ned," they would race out of the dining room while we stayed
at the table drinking coffee, having one more piece of toast,
planning our day. Good old reliable John was in charge back in
our room, and we could relax.

Hotels, restaurants, tea and scones, museums and hushed
cathedrals. If we could manage a trip like this with Ned, we
were all going to be able to have a wonderful life together.

We were full of optimism!

CHAPTER 5

Second Thoughts

After the success of our trip to England, Bill and I decided on an American vacation for the spring of 1977. Washington, D.C.—what could be more American than that? As so often happens, the weather conspired with the fates. It rained and rained and rained. And Ned cried and cried and cried. He was thoroughly miserable, and we could not account for it. Over and over he would say, "The back hurts you. The back hurts you." It seemed at the time to be just another aphasic statement, really meaning something else. But what that something else might be eluded us. There were all the elements that had made our England trip so pleasing to him; hotels and restaurants, museums, constant companionship of both parents and his big brother John, room service for breakfast. It became room service for all meals, for Ned was so unhappy that restaurants were out of the question. We tried but nothing worked. It was cold and wet. The expanse of the Mall seemed endless. We tried to see the chambers of Capitol Hill but were motioned out by the guard, for Ned was too noisy, keeping up a constant sound of misery. We tried for the White House but handicapped kids who were crying were certainly not welcome there. John and I continued on the tour while Bill took Ned out to walk around until we were done. I thought about Mrs. Carter's dedication to the handicapped. Did she know about families like ours? What if there were a time set aside for people who had noisy handicapped kids to visit the White House? I vowed to write to her as soon as I got home. It was time for society to start cooperating with the needs of special children and their families.

We kept at it. Surely Ned would calm down if he got interested in what we were seeing. Up to the top of the Washington Monument. That went fairly well for a while, but then Bill was spotted by a high school group on its senior trip to the nation's capitol. He was waylaid for autographs, and Ned and I went down to circle the monument until he could join us. John came down alone. "Dad will be at least an hour up there," he said. Ned was beginning to cry again, and it was starting to rain again. I had never felt more helpless. We couldn't get back into the monument without standing in line; Ned couldn't be soothed; John was wretched and embarrassed; we couldn't leave because Bill wouldn't know where we were. Bill finally came running up to us. "Let's get out of here!" We tried the Smithsonian, the Library of Congress, the National Gallery. We went back to the hotel, ordered room service, and turned on the television. This was not at all what we had had in mind for our American vacation. But away from the stimulus of public places Ned was a little happier. Washington is a rather challenging city. Perhaps things would be better once we left Washington.

We rented a car and drove off to Mount Vernon. Not too bad there. We toured the house and grounds and Ned ran about on the lawn, and we set off on the next leg of our American vacation with a sense of relief. But it rained every inch of the way to the battlefield at Gettysburg. And poured as we peered through the steamy windshield at the statues and memorials dedicated to the regiments who had fought and died there. We called our friends, Liz and Lou Sauer. We would be late arriving at their house in Philadelphia. That was okay, they would hold dinner.

Ned was out of control by the time we arrived. Liz had known Ned from the beginning, but she had never seen him in this state. He jumped up and down howling in the kitchen and hit the bottom of the bird cage with his head. The bird cage fell over. The parakeets flew about the kitchen. Liz's little girl was in alarmed tears. Ned was crying. I was crying. Liz was crying. And we had been looking forward to the visit so much.

Difficult as it was to have Ned as a houseguest, making "butterflies" out of her beautiful mohair throws, knocking over the bird cage, and making unhappy noises into the night, Liz's real concern was for Ned and the intensity of his suffering. She thought a visit to her pediatrician might help. We took him off the next morning and discussed the problem with the doctor. So Ned was on Ritalin? Perhaps he had outgrown his dosage. A slight increase might help. We went along with it. Anything that might help was more than welcome.

We weren't sure whether the increased Ritalin helped Ned or not, but he did calm down somewhat. Enough for us to take walks about the neighborhood. We strolled along the beautiful streets of Chestnut Hill and past the long stone wall of the Institutes for the Achievement of Human Potential. I had heard of the Institutes. Years ago when John was an infant, I had read an article by Glenn Doman, director of the Institutes, called something like "Teach Your Baby to Be a Genius." We had followed the suggestions in that article for infant stimulation. It had been fun for us and fun for John. We had done the same things for Ned—a crib with slats all around so the baby could see out, bright colors and no shoes, music at certain developmental stages and not at others. I was so enthusiastic about the ideas in the article that I had sent it to Liz when her son, Christopher, had arrived on the scene. I hadn't thought much about the Institutes since those days, and here we were standing outside its grounds. As we walked on, Liz told me of the new experimental work going on there for increasing intelligence in young children. She had enrolled in this program with her daughter and was very caught up in teaching and working with her. Kathryn at two was learning languages, science and math, swimming, and the violin. It was a full-time, exciting project for both of them. The Institutes' principal work was helping the brain-injured, and Liz had seen quite a few children there who reminded her of Ned. She thought Bill and I might be interested in a new and more creative approach to Ned's problems. I hadn't thought of consulting the Institutes about Ned. But Ned wasn't brain-injured. All of the doctors agreed on that. His scans and EEGs were normal. Liz had been spending many days on the grounds of the Institutes and had seen their work with the brain-injured kids. She had begun to think that they might be able to help Christopher, who had a developmental speech problem. He certainly wasn't brain-injured in the ordinary sense of that word either, but the Institutes definition was much broader than that. We strolled on chatting of this and that, admiring the large stone houses and the beginnings of spring. The Institutes was forgotten for the moment.

We drove on to New York. Bill and I had not been there together since our move to California in 1964. And New York was our town. We had reservations at the Plaza, that most remarkable and romantic of New York hotels. We arrived in the rain. Ned was crying. He cried all the way through the imposing entrance. He cried as we skirted the Palm Court. He cried as Bill signed the register. He cried all the way up in the elevator. He cried all the way down the long, long, long corridor. As the bellman unlocked the door to our suite, he looked at us sympathetically and shrugged. "Kids! What do you expect?" We laughed in relief. Well, what did we expect? This was New York. The Plaza Hotel was surely not going to be fazed by a nine-year-old's tears. New York was going to be okay.

We had theater tickets, and Joan and Roger were coming in from Larchmont to go out to dinner and to the theater with us. Joan had arranged a baby-sitter for our boys, and we were off to the real, grown-up New York.

"How was everything?" we asked the sitter on our return.

"Fine," she said, with teenage economy.

"How was everything last night?" we said to John at breakfast.

"Fine," he said. And then, "The lady next door came and said not to make so much noise."

"Oh?"

"And then the man from downstairs came up and said not to swing on the chandelier."

"Oh, no!"

The weather cleared, and Ned was doing slightly better. Bill took the boys to the Statue of Liberty (his turn). And I went shopping. We went to the Central Park Zoo. And we went out to dinner in Greenwich Village.

We found an Italian restaurant that had been there in our day. We tried to settle in but Ned was crying again. He occasionally shouted out a meaningless word or phrase: "Bok!" or "Can I shave?" The restaurant was empty except for us and an elderly gentleman, clearly the proprietor, who sat at a table near the front door, a cup of coffee in front of him. Bill was talking quietly to Ned, trying to soothe him, telling him about all the things around him, speaking gently and lovingly. Ned was inconsolable. If they only would bring the food, I thought. Maybe if he eats, he will stop crying. The waitress became nervous as some other customers entered. She brought us some bread and butter, but she was clearly skeptical of us as patrons. The tension was awful. The tears began to roll down my cheeks. This vacation was hopeless. We just couldn't go on like this. It had all been a terrible mistake. The waitress came over to our table. We would have to leave, we were disturbing the other customers. We started to gather our things together. What were we going to do? We were starving, we would never be able to find a taxi at this time of night, and it had started to rain again. And every other restaurant would be just the same. The old gentleman advanced toward us. Oh, no! I thought. I won't be able to stand it if he starts to lecture us on childrearing. Or if he tells Ned that he is a bad boy. If people only knew. Just because he looks perfectly normal. They don't understand how hard life is for him sometimes.

With economical and authoritative gestures the man motioned us to sit down and take off our coats. "You will stay here for dinner. Bring their food!" he said to the waitress. And to me he said, "You have a wonderful husband. He is a good man. A gentle man." I could only nod my assent and my gratitude for his understanding. The tears were still running down my face. We ate the marvelous, hearty Sicilian food. Everything seemed possible again. New York was remarkable! We had always loved it.

We checked out of the Plaza. They hoped we had had a

pleasant visit. They hoped we would return. They really meant it!

We were off to Connecticut to my mother's house. She plied the boys with food and plenty of hugs, and Ned stopped crying. He ran about under the apple trees, delighting in the physical freedom. We left him behind with his courageous grandparents while we took John to see Hartford and up to New Hampshire to meet my elderly aunts. Finally the time came for us to leave for California. It had all gone very well in Glastonbury. Maybe everything was going to be all right again.

The improvement begun in Connecticut continued after we returned to Pasadena. The nightmare of Washington and New York seemed to be over. Perhaps if we could make some progress on communication, Ned would be able to tell us what he was feeling, and we could avoid future nightmares. We began a new program of language therapy. This meant Ned had therapy four days a week after school: two sessions with Mary Silberzahn and two of language therapy. Dr. Kenneth Knepflar, the speech-language pathologist, was a very experienced person. He worked skillfully with Ned and designed a language stimulation program for us to carry out at home. I made a book for Ned with favorite snapshots and took others of him engaged in his everyday activities: carrying in the groceries, putting his laundry in the basket, getting dressed, making pancakes, husking corn, standing up on the swing. Under the pictures Dr. Knepflar wrote appropriate sentences based on the vocabulary Ned had already acquired: "I am carrying in the groceries." "I kiss Daddy good-bye." He added words Ned was to strive for: possessive pronouns—"I am tying *my* shoes"; emotional words—"I am *happy* to see Daddy." It was interesting and gentle and Ned liked it.

Meanwhile, my thoughts kept returning to the discussions I had had with Liz as we walked around Chestnut Hill. I phoned her and we discussed the Institutes again. "I can't get it out of my mind. Perhaps we should look into what they might have to offer Ned." Liz had been thinking about it too, and she sent me Glenn Doman's book, *What to Do About Your Brain-Injured Child*. I read it, fascinated. The term "brain-injured," as he defined it, included not merely injury due to accident but even undetectable injury, or injury due to illness, or injury before birth, which caused the problems that were called by a multitude of names by the bulk of professionals. The Institutes didn't worry too much about labels; they were all "hurt kids." Possibly in the terms of the Institutes, Ned was brain-injured. Perhaps a new approach would help our child. What did we have to lose? In spite of all we had tried to do for him, it hadn't been enough. Teachers, doctors, and therapists kept trying with him, but it wasn't enough. The professionals we had been working with didn't have enough of the answers. I wrote to the Institutes.

Pasadena, California
May 1, 1977

Miss Gretchen Kerr
The Institutes for the Achievement of Human Potential
8801 Stenton Ave.
Philadelphia, Pa. 19118

Dear Miss Kerr:
I have just finished reading Glenn Doman's book, What to Do About Your Brain-Injured Child, *which was sent to me by my friend Elizabeth Sauer, who has two children in Institutes programs. She sent me the book because she is familiar with our long and anguished search for help for our nine-year-old son, Ned.*

I will outline for you the steps we have been through in this search so that you will be able to answer my obvious question.

1. Ned was quite different from his older brother from the very beginning (six weeks old when we adopted him). He was less responsive and stiff bodily.

2. The pediatrician discovered at three months that Ned's eyes weren't tracking properly. The eyes were corrected through therapy, and Ned became much more responsive and laughed for the first time.

3. He was still different in an almost indefinable way, but he progressed at a seemingly normal rate—doing everything at the average (according to Spock) time or earlier. He seemed to be exceptionally bright although his language development was strange. He couldn't (at age two and a half) answer the question "What is your name?" but he knew all of the flags of the United Nations, could pick out a tune on the piano, knew all the plants in our garden and could identify them by their foliage wherever he saw them. He could read quite a few words, count forward and backward, spell, write his name, etc. He didn't develop any relationships with children (except his brother), although he had some favorite adults.

4. We still had a nagging feeling that something was wrong but our doctor was reassuring in the way that we now recognize as classic.

5. Ned started nursery school—the same excellent school his brother had attended and for which we had great respect. After a few months the director of the school asked for a conference. She told me that she was very concerned about Ned. She said that he was the brightest child she had ever had in thirty years of running a nursery school. His building with blocks was extraordinary and elaborate, he could spell and read many words, his flag trick, etc. However, Ned did not interact with other children unless he pulled their hair, and he did this not in an emotional way but as if they were mere objects. She suggested that we see a psychologist.

6. We did. He felt that we were doing "all the right things" but that Ned was mentally retarded and should be taken out of school—too challenging for him. We did that and all the children in his class sent him farewell cards. Ned read all of their names aloud to us. (He was three and a half at this time.)

7. After thinking this step over for a while, I became very dissatisfied and felt I had to search further for an answer.

8. I called UCLA and made an appointment for Ned with the department of pediatric neurology. Diagnosis: atypical with autistic tendencies, normal intelligence. Needs special education.

9. I visited, with Ned, a school for special education in our area and talked with the director. She felt special-ed was not indicated as Ned was "certainly not autistic" and was much too normal. She recommended a specialist, a pediatrician who works only with developmentally disabled children.

10. *This doctor found Ned to have above average intelligence and a lag in motor development and diagnosed him as expressive aphasic. She felt that he might normalize by age five and be able to go to regular school. She recommended a therapeutic nursery school. At this point his language was still undeveloped, he spent hours throwing small objects, and was still not making much social contact.*

11. *The therapeutic nursery school was a disastrous step. Ned was physically manipulated through his day so that he could be "taught" how to hang up his coat, for example, which he had been doing for years. He was asked to throw things against the wall and say, "I'm mad," when he pulled hair. This all seemed pointless to us. We were asked to sit behind a magic mirror to learn how to deal with Ned. We were getting very nervous by this time.*

12. *Next, public school aphasic kindergarten, where he was expected to sit at a desk and learn. He couldn't, and his behavior grew worse. He started stripping in the school bus and throwing his clothes out the window. He was excluded from school and appointed a home teacher. (He was five and a half at this point.)*

(Throughout all of this there were bizarre behaviors, some blessedly temporary—like stripping and a brief period of licking the pavement. Others—throwing, shredding, making strange noises, laughing uncontrollably and irrelevantly—have continued on and off to the present.)

13. *The home teacher came expecting a "slow learner." She found Ned quick to learn and left many educational toys for him to play with. He did this with my help and seemed to make progress and to enjoy himself. Even his breathing changed as he concentrated on his learning tasks.*

14. *School again. This time a private special-ed day school. Their analysis before admitting him: Emotionally disturbed and mentally retarded.*

15. *Ned has been at this school for more than three years now and there have been ups and downs in my attitude about the school. I am down at the moment because Ned's present teacher feels that he can't teach Ned or get him to focus. No effort is being made on reading. I am discouraged.*

16. *In the past three years we have also tried megavitamin therapy and a special diet, which helped for about two years and*

then didn't seem to help any more. At one point our doctor thought Ned might be having seizures, but one of the medications prescribed provoked a severe reaction (violence, loss of balance, destructiveness) from which it took eight months to fully recover. At the moment, he has no anticonvulsants but he is on Ritalin, which has helped reduce a severe tooth-grinding problem.

17. Through these last three years, Ned has been receiving occupational therapy for sensory integration, and this is the one bright spot in this whole gloomy picture. I attribute any progress he has made to this therapy. For example, he now has a more relaxed and normal body—walks and runs with opposition. His interest in communication has grown. His babbling to himself has turned into talking to himself. Yet we are not satisfied. He still has limited vocabulary and forgets words that he "knows." He has never used "how" or "why" and uses few pronouns. He relates very little to other children except his brother. He becomes confused easily and covers his eyes and ears to shut out too much stimulation. He plays alone but enjoys our company. None of this is enough.

We met last year with a psychiatrist who was evaluating Ned for the California Regional Center (the agency responsible for programs for the developmentally disabled in our state). His parting words to us were, "Look, he's autistic. You're doing everything that can be done. You won't need any help from us until you decide to institutionalize him."

But I cannot think calmly of a future with Ned in a mental institution. True, we have tried to do everything that can be done but there must be more we can do for him.

Glenn Doman's book has made me think that perhaps the Institutes in Philadelphia can tell us what that more is. My obvious question: Can the Institutes evaluate Ned and help us with a home program for him? How do we go about applying? We can be available to come to Philadelphia on very short notice.

Very truly yours,
Barbara O. Christopher

I bought Glenn Doman's book, *How to Teach Your Baby to Read.* I would try some of the Institutes ideas and see if I could make Ned's life a little more interesting. It went well and he did learn quickly, as usual.

Pasadena, California
May 21, 1977

Dear Grandma and Grandpa Jim,

I've started collecting stamps. I'm putting my stamps into my albums right now. Please send me some of the interesting stamps that you get on your mail. Our school is going to start a stamp club that I will be in.

The Red Sox are doing pretty well (18-15 .545). Are my Dodgers doing it? (30-9 .763). One of the best starts ever. 11½ games in front of Cincinnati and 12½ in front of Houston. Right now they have the biggest lead since coming to L.A. The Bosox are only 1 game behind New York and ½ behind Baltimore. But Milwaukee is just ½ behind the Bosox.

Our Little League team (Pirates) are in 2nd place behind the Dodgers. I'm playing third regularly. We play the 4th place Giants tomorrow.

Pepper is fine and I have started taking him on a walk more often. We got him a new bowl because the other got lost somewhere.

Dad has been busy doing things but "M*A*S*H" doesn't start again until July.

Mom has started teaching Ned how to read and he is coming along GREAT! Sometimes he closes his eyes and guesses. But he can read most of his words if he looks at them.

Don't forget to send some stamps you get.

OXOXXOO
Love,
John Christopher

PS The clock that Grandma Louise and Grandpa Chris sent is neat and you should see it.

We heard from the Institutes. There was nothing in our letter that would preclude Ned as a possible candidate for an

Institutes program. There were some things we should understand before applying: There would be about a one-year wait for an appointment. (Oh, dear!) Next, the appointment for the initial evaluation would require five days and five evenings. And both parents must be there. (That presented some problems. How was Bill ever to promise a whole working week of availability? Well, we would face that later.) The letter explained that the entire staff of the Institutes would be involved in evaluation: The first two days would be used to test and observe Ned and determine whether or not he could benefit from the program. If Ned were not accepted, there would be no charge and we would return home. (That struck us as very fair.) If Ned were accepted, we would have two days of lectures and demonstrations to teach us about brain injury and how the brain functions and grows. On the fifth day we would be taught exactly how to do the program designed specifically for Ned. We would have to find a place to stay. (We were lucky there; we had friends, dear friends, within walking distance.) The total charge for the entire service including all tests, all teaching, all meals for the three of us, and all programming was $450. (Fantastic!) We were to understand that the program would be a home program designed by the Institutes and carried out by us at home. There would be periodic return visits to the Institutes for reevaluation and reprogramming. We should send any additional information along with a request for an appointment.

I took a deep breath and sat at my desk to look through the old reports in my rather fat, disorganized file labeled "Ned." So much had been tried, so little had really helped; or rather, the help had been inadequate to the need.

I read Dr. Salley's report on her initial evaluation. Five and a half years ago this highly respected professional had seen Ned as fairly normal with an emotional disorder. Time had not proven her optimistic predictions of normalcy to be accurate, but when she made them, her observations had seemed correct. We had all been so wrong, so very wrong in our expectations. Dr. Salley's description of Ned presented some interesting contrasts to his present situation. There was no question that he had grown in social awareness and contact, but in relationship to his chronological age he had actually lost ground. Dr. Salley had evaluated him at three and a half as being at an eighteen-month level socially. But giving him every benefit of doubt, I could not honestly appraise his current social behavior at any higher than a three-year-old level. That put him six years behind a normal child, a frightening gap. When I read Dr. Salley's description of Ned's fine-motor and desk skills, I had to admit very little had changed and what had been amazing block building and writing at that time was far from what is expected of a nine-year-old. Ned was also still immature in the gross-motor area. Although he was strong and agile, he had only recently begun to swing his arms when walking or running. As for language, no one could call Ned's language within normal limits now. And it was not, as Dr. Salley had originally thought, a question of motivation, as he sometimes tried very hard to communicate but couldn't remember the appropriate words. I felt overwhelmed.

I turned to the reports from Dubnoff for the three and a half years Ned had been enrolled there. The early reports sounded quite good. Through his initial experience with Betty Fried and his two years in Robin's class, Ned showed continual improvement. There had been a few puzzling episodes. Robin had written that Ned had had a period when he forgot how to write some of the letters of the alphabet. And he had briefly forgotten how to tie his shoes. That had been a great frustration to Ned. He worked and worked to relearn, and with as much help as he would let us give him, he did relearn in a few weeks. And there had been a period when he had given up much of his climbing and acrobatics. But he was back to doing all of that. Somewhat reassuring, I thought. Comparing Robin's reports with those of his current teacher, there was no doubt that Ned's school performance was not what it had been. I had recently come to view his current Dubnoff program as impoverished in content and too permissive in structure, and I was hoping for a far superior one next year. The latest Dubnoff report described his present school day: Ned would enter the classroom in the morning without greeting anyone. His first act would be to get his "cape," a large piece of sheeting, and drape it around his shoulders. He didn't play with other children but did watch them closely. He liked to roll a pencil about on the desk top or tear paper. He sat in the circle with the group but limited his participation to one-word answers. His work in class consisted of drawing mazes, doing four-piece puzzles, sorting alphabet letters, writing numbers, finger painting, building block patterns, and doing hand games such as pat-a-cake. The teacher said that Ned liked to be chased as a reward and that from time to time he would play catch, but he spent most of his day engaged in socially inappropriate self-stimulatory behaviors. Oh, dear!

I turned to a recent report from Dr. Knepflar. It was a very complete and accurate picture of Ned's language. And, I commented to myself, he has made considerable progress since this report. There was also a note I had sent to Dr. Knepflar quite recently:

To: Dr. Knepflar
Re: Ned's reaction to his last session with Frank

When Ned saw Frank on Friday, he was extremely uncooperative. When the session ended I spoke to Ned very severely and told him that I was very angry with him and expressed the necessity of his "doing his work" in future sessions.

Ned became very subdued and in the car going home kept saying, "Hi," and, "Hold my hand." I responded very coldly and told him repeatedly that I was very annoyed and that he had not done his work and that I did not feel like holding his hand or saying "hi" to him.

When we got home, Ned went into the house before me, and when I went inside a few minutes later, he was sitting in a little corner chair that used to be his "thinking" chair. (We used to ask him to sit and think about our rules when he had misbehaved.) The following conversation ensued:

Ned: I'm very disappointed in you. [Meaning the reverse.]
Me: Yes, Ned. I'm very disappointed. I want you to be a good boy when you go to Dr. Knepflar's office.
Ned: I'm very cross with you.

Me: Yes, Ned, I am cross. Why is Mommy cross?
Ned: Don't tear leaves. Don't hit Frank. Don't turn off the
light. Don't kick the bed. [Meaning couch.] Don't jump up and
down on the bed. Don't touch the light.
Me: That's right, Ned. What are you supposed to do at Dr.
Knepflar's office?
Ned: Do your work.
Me: Yes, you must do your work.
Ned: Sit in your chair and do your work.
We went on like this for a while. When I felt it was time for a
change, I suggested that he set the table for dinner. He did so but
kept returning to the old subject, asking for hugs. I gave him lots
of hugs, and we talked of his complete reformation in future. Ned
was more truly contrite than I have ever seen him and more verbal
about his own behavior than I have heard.

Barbara Christopher

When did he roll over? When did he sit up? Everyone else
had wanted the answers to these questions; I supposed that the
Institutes would too. I took another deep breath, searched my
records, and made a list of developmental steps for the
Institutes. I sent off as much additional information as I could
compile at home, requested an appointment, and sat back to
wait for an answer. Perhaps a year from now we would be on a
whole new approach. That, at least, sounded optimistic.

The letter finally came. Our appointment was for October 16,
1978. Sixteen months! That was quite a wait for a desperate
family. Meanwhile we had to soldier on with everyday life.
Ned would continue to attend Dubnoff; he would continue his
occupational therapy; he would continue his language
therapy; he would continue to work on his reading at home; he
would continue with Ritalin.

Ned's behavior began to worsen; there was more crying,
more agitation. We took him to see Dr. Salley. She wasn't sure
what had gone wrong, and she wanted some consultations.
We were to go back to the neurologist, and she also wanted us
to see a psychiatrist. Perhaps Ned had had a psychotic break.

The neurologist increased his Ritalin and the psychiatrist suggested psychotherapeutic sessions in which he would meet privately with Ned to talk with him. (What!) Let's be conservative, Dr. Salley said. Let's see how he does on the Ritalin increase.

Summer arrived, and we were going back to Balboa. That had always been Ned's favorite place in the world. Sand cakes and frozen bananas. The Fun Zone, the ferry, the ferris wheel. The sun and the sea. Lazy times. We were optimistic that a return to such happy scenes would help Ned. He was still crying a lot, and his behavior had become increasingly bizarre. We had found him on the roof of our house. We had coaxed him down from very high up on our palm tree. We were constantly heading him off as he darted toward the potted plants, intending to drop them on the bricks and watch them break. He was shredding leaves with great fury. His agitation was increasing. But surely Balboa, that most relaxed place, would help.

It didn't. On a walk to buy a frozen banana Ned threw himself down on the street in the middle of traffic and began to lick the pavement. What were we going to do? Whatever were we going to do?

Bill was commuting from the beach to Twentieth Century Fox each day for shooting. I did my best to keep Ned amused in his absence. I took the boys across on the ferry. We had been invited to have dinner with my friend Beth and her children. We sat on the sand, and John played with the other kids. It was peaceful. But Ned wasn't joining in. He was lying in the sand; he was crying. It was time to go in for dinner. John had walked down the beach and sat staring at the water. He stood up and marched resolutely toward us and announced that he was going back to our cottage. He did not want to stay for dinner. "Okay," I said, "here's the key and a dime for the ferry." Ned and I would stay. Food usually helped Ned, and he had stopped crying for the moment. Beth, in her understanding way, got dinner right on. We ate and went home to see John. "What's the matter?" I asked.

"I couldn't stand it. All the other kids were playing and my brother was lying in the sand crying."

I understood. My heart was breaking too. If Balboa couldn't

work its magic on Ned, no place could. We would have to look elsewhere for magic.

Somehow we got through the rest of vacation and the rest of summer. But when Ned returned to Dubnoff for the fall, it was obvious that something had to be done. He was unmanageable in class, and he wasn't learning. He could learn at home on the reading program I had started, but in class he was inattentive. He was difficult on the drive over to school, noisy and restless. And things were getting worse.

We had a desperate meeting with Dr. Salley. We outlined all that was happening. Ned was often awake until two or three in the morning, rocking, getting up, laughing maniacally. He was grinding his teeth with a fury and sometimes attempted to bite or pinch. He looked very thin. Ned had not gained weight in two years although he had grown three inches. He was hungry all the time. He was throwing himself on his knees everywhere, even on cement, and we were afraid he would injure himself. He seemed to feel no pain. He had developed a routine of compulsive touching: walls, fences, doorknobs. He persisted in asking his favorite nonsense question, "Can I shave?" and shouting out, "Bok!" These exclamations were strangely inflected and couldn't be interrupted. If anyone responded with a logical, "You don't need to shave, Ned—you are only nine years old," he looked bewildered, as if he didn't understand that he had said anything. He was crying without apparent reason, a tearless crying so loud and prolonged that he sometimes lost his voice, crying for hours unrelieved. He was sometimes very withdrawn and would lie with his blanket around him clutching his head. He was breaking his toys, tearing books, dropping flower pots. He seemed to have superhuman strength. He was extremely sensitive and would cover his eyes and ears and couldn't bear to be touched. He seemed to be in anguish. He had no pleasures, no longer enjoyed the things he had always loved: restaurants, favorite foods, the beach. He was undressing in public. He was sitting or lying in the street. What was more, he was interfering with John. John was afraid of Ned when he became wild, and he was having difficulty protecting his possessions. John had always been so protective of Ned, had always been able to manage

Ned so well. Now there were frustrations and many tears and depression. John wouldn't fight back; he was too sensitive for that. But he couldn't go on much longer like this. None of us could.

Dr. Salley thought that perhaps Ned had begun to react adversely to Ritalin. She wanted him off Ritalin and as soon as possible. It would have to be done in the hospital, and she wanted him at UCLA Medical Center.

At UCLA Ned was so active that the hospital required him to be tied in his bed and insisted that he have private nurses around the clock. It would take about a week for his Ritalin to be eliminated. But it didn't take long before we knew that Dr. Salley's hunch was right. As we watched day after day, we saw our old Ned reemerge. He stopped crying. He regained his healthy appearance. He became interested in everything. I brought his reading materials to the hospital and entertained him. Meanwhile Dr. Salley had begun to think that Ned should be admitted to the Neuropsychiatric Institute (NPI) at UCLA for further evaluation. She wanted expert opinion on Ned. She wanted to know what was going on with him neurologically and also to get some guidance on his education. NPI was the best there was, she said. Teams of doctors began to march into his room to determine whether or not Ned should be admitted to NPI. They didn't introduce themselves. They discussed Ned freely in front of him and us. They weren't interested when I tried to give something of the history of what had been going on. But eventually the decision was made that they would accept him.

Ned was moved to the autism ward. We, as parents, were not welcome. There was to be no dropping in. We could come by appointment only. We would be expected to meet weekly with the psychiatrist. We would take Ned home on weekends. We brought him his clothes and toys. We brought him some Neosporin ointment for the small spot of eczema behind his ear. We brought his reading materials. We were to come back next week.

When we picked Ned up on Saturday morning for his first weekend home visit, he was dressed in unfamiliar clothing. One of the nurses explained that he had been wetting himself, and he had no clean clothes.

"But all the other kids in the unit are wearing his clothes."

"Yes," she said, "Ned has such cute clothes. The other kids love them."

"I can't understand his wetting himself. He has been toilet-trained since he was two and a half."

"Well, you would never know it here."

"Has a urologist been consulted?"

"You will have to ask the doctor about that."

"And what about that eczema behind his ear? It has spread across half of his head and is oozing."

"I'll mention it to the doctor. Have a nice weekend, Ned. See you tomorrow night."

"No UCLA!"

Ned was very happy to be home. He was back to himself, no longer crying all the time. He was our old Ned. Except that he now wet himself. I cleaned his head and put ointment on it. I put him to sleep in his own bed; he was happy and relaxed. But I didn't want him to think that he didn't have to go back. "Once upon a time there was a little boy named Ned. He lived with his mommy and his daddy and his big brother John in a nice house in Pasadena. Once he was having a hard time and the doctor thought he should go to the hospital at UCLA . . ."

"No UCLA!"

" . . . but he could come home on the weekends. Everyone loved to have Ned come home for the weekend, and soon he would be able to come home all the time. But not right away."

"The end," said Ned.

"Good night, Ned."

"Good night, Mommy."

Each weekend we would drive to UCLA to pick Ned up, and each weekend it grew harder to take him back. Was NPI really necessary? We missed Ned terribly. His reaction to Ritalin had been the problem and that was all taken care of now. Shouldn't we just go on as we had before? Were we doing the right thing? Had we ever done the right thing?

I spent many days with Leona. She and Bob lived close to UCLA. I would stop off at her house and over countless cups of tea pour out my worries to her. She wanted me to meet a friend of theirs who also had an autistic child, a young man who lived in an institution but who was able to come home now and then to visit his mother. During lunch I told the friend about Ned. "Give him up," she said. "You won't be able to really help him, and it will tear you apart." But we couldn't follow this advice. We had to keep trying.

The weeks dragged on at NPI. We were desperate and confused. I arrived home one afternoon just as Bill was pulling into the driveway, home from the studio. "Guess what?" he called. "Prince Charles is going to visit the set. We're invited to a luncheon to meet him. I'm not sure you'll want to go with all that we have going on."

"Are you kidding? A chance to meet the Prince of Wales, the world's most eligible bachelor, the descendant of William the Conqueror? I'll be there!" We were both there, along with four hundred other honored guests, to meet the prince—absolutely the most glamorous of afternoons. Everyone in Hollywood was there, Cary Grant and Lauren Bacall, but every eye was on Prince Charles. This was certainly a break in the routine of driving to NPI to pick up or deliver Ned or to have a conference with the psychiatrist. But it was more than just a break. We had to keep some part of ourselves separate from the problems that threatened our happiness. "It is well to have as many holds upon happiness as possible."

The following day we met with the psychiatrist. He recommended that we get rid of Ned. We had tried with Ned, but he had gone as far as he could go. We had adopted this child; we had reached into the barrel and had pulled out a rotten apple. It was time to realize this and to relinquish him to the state. Then we could get on with working on our own lives. And besides, if we relinquished him, we would be able to write him out of our will; we would have no more financial responsibility. Ned was classically autistic. Ned had no future. His only strong point was that he was good-looking and likable. Had he said anything to upset me? Here was a Kleenex.

We drove home on the freeway, tears and rage alternating with moments of helpless laughter at the absurd contrasts these two days had offered. Yesterday we had shaken the hand of the heir to the throne of the United Kingdom of Great Britain. We had sat at a glamorous luncheon and heard his witty speech. Today we had actually been presented with the craven suggestion that we might like to save money and trouble by getting rid of the child we dearly loved!

We arrived home and sat in the garden to have a cup of tea and consider the future. The liquidambars were beginning to turn, the sasanquas were in full bloom, and some of the early bulbs were poking shoots through the earth with their annual promise of beauty. "It is well to have as many holds upon happiness as possible."

We took Ned out of NPI. We brought him home. It had been a terrible ordeal but one good thing had come out of the experience. Although the psychiatrist didn't think there was much hope for Ned, he had found a solution to a long-standing problem. Ned had begun years ago to thrust out his jaw, covering his upper teeth with his lower. Our dentist had recommended an orthodontist. But the orthodontist hadn't wanted to work with Ned. He thought that Ned would probably remove the braces, and besides, was it really worth it for a child like Ned? What was it going to matter? The psychiatrist at NPI felt differently. "How can you expect him to develop his language when he can't close his mouth properly?" he said, and he saw to it that Ned was examined at the clinic for special children at UCLA Dental School. A course of orthodontia was begun immediately. Now that NPI was over, the dentistry would continue. The necessary correction wasn't very great; it would only take a few months. For his visits Ned was put into a papoose, a comfortable restraint that kept him wrapped up so he couldn't get his hands in the way. He didn't mind going to the dental clinic, and he liked the pretty assistants there, but "No UCLA!" burst out of him at the sight of the entrance to NPI.

Ned was back home, back at Dubnoff, back with Mary Silberzahn, back with Dr. Knepflar. We had Thanksgiving with Bob and Leona, and Ned was well behaved. His old self. He began to move forward again. But he was still wetting himself. The NPI psychiatrist had told us that Ned would never get over that. "He is wetting himself because he is angry at you. Once they lose their bladder control, they don't tend to get it back."

This was pretty discouraging. Our great little boy who had

trained himself at two was now wet all the time. He had gone into NPI, "the best there was," and he had come out wet. He took two or three changes with him to school each day. But it was disheartening to all of us and puzzling to Ned. He would look down at his wet jeans and go into his room and change.

We thought the psychiatrist had been wrong about most things; perhaps he was wrong about bladder control. We took Ned to see our friend Grady Harp, a urologist. Grady had the answer. Ritalin enhances the pathway from the bladder to the brain. When you take a child off Ritalin who has been on it for some time, he doesn't get the signal that his bladder is full. There was a medication we could try. It would help Ned receive the correct messages, and he would be slowly weaned from that medication. It worked. Soon Ned was dry all the time again. How was it, we asked ourselves, that the hospital where Ned had been sent to take him off Ritalin didn't know this? How was it that the psychiatrist thought that this regression was for life?

My mother and Jim came for the holidays. We all went out together dressed up for New Year's Eve dinner, Ned in a turtleneck shirt and John's outgrown blazer, John in a much-hated necktie. We had a party for the rose parade, twenty adults and seventeen children. Life was getting better again.

A letter came. There had been a cancellation at the Institutes. Could we make an appointment in April of 1978? Could we! Happy New Year!

CHAPTER 6

Taking Over

I know what you want. You want your child to be well."
Barbara and I were sitting in the auditorium at the Institutes
for the Achievement of Human Potential. We had completed
the initial two days of testing by this time, and it had been
determined that Ned was a candidate for an Institutes
program. They had been exhausting and fascinating days
during which we had gone through a detailed history of Ned's
life with each of the Institutes departments. The questions had
gone far beyond the ones we were so used to: When did he roll
over? When did he sit up? Never before had we talked so
extensively about our life with Ned. Never before had we been
asked what we thought the problem was. In these interviews,
time was of no importance. The staff had been interested in all
we had to say.

Ned was with us throughout all of these interviews, and
while we talked, the staff observed him, stopping occasionally
for gentle testing. He was asked to perform a series of tasks:
Reach into a bag and identify objects he found there by
touch—he couldn't do that at all. Hop on one foot—that he was
terrific at. They took measurements of his skull and chest as
well as his height and weight. They measured his breathing
and his responses to sound and light. He had a complete
physical. And so on throughout two full days.

During the waiting period between interviews, we sat in a
large circular room in the Children's Center with all the other
parents and kids who, like us, were there for the first time.
There were chairs around the edge of the room and the floor

was heavily padded. Each day at the Institutes was a long one, twelve or sixteen hours (even longer for the staff, who sat in meetings after the families had gone for the night). During the periods of waiting, we had begun to know the other families who were going through the same process. We were all members of a class, or "kumi" as it was called. (The Institutes used this Japanese word.) If we did go on an Institutes program, we would remain in the same kumi on return visits. At first we sat rather quietly, looking at each other's children, noticing what was different about them, reluctant to ask questions. But as the hours wore on, we became acquainted, chatting about our experiences in raising handicapped children, or "hurt kids" as we were beginning to call them. They had many different kinds of problems. Some were completely immobile, lying on the padded floor; others were Down's syndrome kids; one little boy was extremely hyperactive. Most of the children had been born with their conditions, but a few were victims of illness or accident. The parents were from all kinds of backgrounds: politicians, laborers, educators, businessmen, farmers. They were from all over the United States and from Italy and Zambia and Australia and New Zealand. But we were finding that, different though we might be, we had a great deal in common. We all had been frustrated by conventional approaches to our children; we all believed that more could be done; we all thought that the Institutes might have the answers that no one else had been able to provide. And we were all excited and a little startled at what we were experiencing.

Now, as the parents attended two full days of lectures, the staff took charge of Ned and the other kids in our kumi, caring for them, observing and working with them, beginning to form conclusions about appropriate treatment. We had been told to bring blankets to the lecture hall. There would be twelve hours of lectures each day, and the auditorium was kept very cold in order to keep us alert. There was a ten-minute break each hour, and we would go out into the lobby and have some coffee or soup or a sandwich—healthy and simple food, enough to keep us going, not enough to make us drowsy.

The lectures were to instruct us on the theories and methods of the Institutes. Now Glenn Doman was standing before us, and he said the words that made us know we were in the right place. "I know what you want. You want your child to be well." Such a simple statement, and the most understanding one we had heard from all the many, many professionals we had encountered. He went on to say that he had noticed through the years that parents would claim, "All we want is for Danny to walk," but as soon as Danny was walking they wanted him to be able to tie his shoes. We understood exactly what he meant. How many times professionals had asked us, "What do you want for Ned? What do you expect him to be?" What an impossible question! I had only one thought about Ned's future, that he should get better. And how could I really want anything but complete normalcy? We wanted Ned to be well, to be normal. I don't mean we actually expected normalcy to happen for Ned; we had reluctantly come to accept the idea that it would not, that normalcy would be too much of a miracle. Although we refused to accept the pessimistic view expressed at NPI, we wanted to be realistic. Nevertheless, until Ned was doing all the things a normal child could do, until the day came that Ned could be called normal, we would not be satisfied. We kept listening.

Glenn Doman said another thing that we liked: "You are the world's greatest expert on your child." At last! A professional was telling us that our experience counted for something, that nearly ten years of intimate contact with this person called Ned had given us insights that no one else could have, and what is more, that his love for us meant that we could reach him when no one else could, that we might be the most effective therapists possible.

We listened and listened while one after another of the staff lectured us on the work of the Institutes. We learned the whys of the treatments we would be expected to carry out as part of our child's program. The underlying approach was developmental. It seemed simple enough: that each individual goes through certain necessary stages of development; that each stage in development must be experienced to prepare the brain for the demands of the next stage; that the history of each individual is a restatement of the development of the entire human race. All Institutes treatment is based on the idea that the hurt brain can be stimulated by retracing earlier stages of motor development, which may have been missed or experienced inadequately or lost through accident or illness. As a hurt individual goes through the physical activities of normal development, his brain can be changed from an imperfectly functioning one to a normally functioning one, or at least brought closer. Our children would be analyzed as to where they fit on the developmental scale, and each child would be assigned treatments based on his developmental level. It all sounded so logical and interesting and concrete.

After hearing about the theoretical basis of the Institutes approach to treatment, we heard lectures on the treatments themselves. There was crawling on the belly. In a normal infant crawling occurs when the brain is just beginning to organize the body it has charge of. We learned that a normal crawling pattern is especially important. And if our kids could move at all, they would probably be assigned a lot of crawling. I had done some crawling when I was in the army, and I recalled how difficult it was for some men. Of course, we all did it once, I thought, though I couldn't remember much about Ned's crawl.

Creeping on the hands and knees is the next stage of motor development, and like crawling, it is an important Institutes treatment. So, the kids would need to crawl and they would need to creep and they would need to do it right. The Institutes have a treatment for that too—patterning. Patterning is moving the arms, legs, and head of a disabled person through a normal pattern of body movement. It is a way of telling the brain, "Here's how you do it."

Another treatment activity is brachiation. This is traveling along a horizontal ladder, hand over hand, swinging like an ape. And although we may never have done it as a developmental step in our own lives, there is a logic to brachiation in terms of the development of the race as a whole.

Some lectures emphasized the need to give the hurt brain the best possible environment. This means the best nutrition, and we heard a lot about diet and vitamins. And the brain doesn't just need the right food, it needs oxygen. The Institutes method of increasing oxygen to the brain is to place a small mask over the nose and mouth for a specified number of seconds. During this time exhaled breath is reinhaled, steadily increasing the carbon dioxide content in the bloodstream. This causes the blood vessels in the brain to dilate; the brain gets a larger volume of blood and a much larger supply of oxygen. Wearing the mask causes increasingly deeper breathing, giving the lungs a strenuous workout. Both breathing and brain benefit.

We went on to hear about "frequency, intensity, and duration." These were the key words of every Institutes treatment. Each treatment had its prescribed frequency. Masking, for example, was often scheduled every seven minutes of a child's waking day. Intensity, too, was prescribed. One child might need the gentlest of tactile stimulation, another to be bombarded with sensory input. Duration might be hours of creeping or a split-second reading lesson. It all began to sound very, very challenging.

Each evening we went back to Liz and Lou's house with our minds crammed full of new ideas and sat up half the night talking about how remarkable and different it all was. We had seen the brain-injured students who were living on the grounds of the Institutes, and we had marveled at their incredibly arduous physical activities. We had also seen demonstrations of skill and virtuosity by the little well kids who were part of the experimental intelligence program. The whole place, innovative and exciting, was also somewhat intimidating. It was wonderful to think that we could take over Ned's life and accomplish what the professionals could not, but we were terrified by the thought of turning our home into a workplace for repairing Ned's brain. We didn't know exactly what the Institutes would require of the Christopher family, but we had seen and heard enough to know that it would be a tremendous amount of work.

"Do you think they'll want Ned to mask every seven minutes?"

"Surely not. There isn't anything wrong with Ned's breathing."

"I don't think we'll have to pattern, do you? After all, Ned is completely mobile. Some of these kids can't move at all. They're the ones who'll need patterning."

We speculated, wondering and a little afraid of what was going to be asked of us.

On the final day of our five-day appointment, we gathered once more in the Children's Center and were given the home programs for our kids. Once more we made the rounds of staff members, going from office to office, getting instructions on exactly how to do each treatment and what records we were to keep. There were demonstrations and opportunities to practice. We were given diagrams and references for specific materials we would need. We were given the exact frequency, intensity, and duration of each treatment. We had the starting points and the goals, the impossible goals, that we were to strive for in the next three months.

Of course, Ned was to crawl. His goal was to be able to crawl 500 yards per day in a one-hour non-stop session. This made basic training sound easy. Then he was to creep. The goal: 2,500 yards per day in two one-hour sessions. Almost a mile and a half on the hands and knees!

Ned was to be patterned after all. He was mobile, but his style of crawling, the rhythm of his creep, and even his way of walking and running were not perfect enough for the standards of these exacting people. Eight times a day, for stretches of five minutes each, he would lie on a table while three people moved him through the pattern of a perfect crawl. Well, I thought, we're lucky John is a good athletic specimen; we'll need his help with this one. That is, if we actually decide to go ahead with all of this. Both Barbara and I were feeling a little dazed by this time.

Ned was to be off his feet except one hour a day. He was going to live on his hands and knees. That struck me as an unusual but wonderful idea. On the floor he would not be able to engage in all his aimless jumping and running about. Perhaps he would even give up some of his other meaningless movement, like shaking his head from side to side. But how could we possibly prevent him from getting up? There would be no way that Ned, who loved to run about, would put up with staying on the floor all day. It would never work. "Don't worry," we were told, "just try it."

Ned was to be masked every seven minutes for exactly one

minute except when he was eating or during heavy physical exertion. Better breathing would not only provide better nutrition for his brain, but increased lung capacity would give him the breath needed for longer sentences, better language. There were to be forty maskings per day. Every seven minutes! How could we ever do that and have time for anything else? "It soon becomes automatic," we were told with a smile.

Ned was to brachiate. His goal: thirty round trips daily on a fifteen-foot ladder. We had seen the long, high brachiation ladders that were used by the resident students, and I had tried them out for fun myself. I had always enjoyed this exercise as a kid. Although Ned had never shown much interest in such organized activity, he loved to hang by his arms from the chinning bar I had installed in his bedroom doorway. Perhaps I could teach him to brachiate. I tried not to worry about all those round trips.

Ned was to have a high-protein diet with plenty of whole grains, fresh fruits and vegetables, and no refined sugars at all (back to the sugar-free life; we had let that lapse after our trip to England). All this was to be supplemented by megavitamins. We were to restrict his intake of fluids. He was to have tactile stimulation: a cold rinse in the shower and rubdowns with rough towels.

Finally, there was the intelligence program. Ned would have one hundred reading words and twenty-five phrases or sentences presented to him every day. They would be printed on cards in red letters at least one inch high, the words in groups of ten, the sentences in groups of five. We were to read them aloud, showing them very quickly, fifteen seconds for a group of cards. He would see each group three times a day for five days and then not see it again. Each day we were to retire a group of words and a group of sentences and replace them with new ones. We would have to keep up a constant flow of new materials, hundreds of word cards, hundreds of sentence cards. How could we ever do it? Not to mention keeping track of it all. But Barbara is a great organizer. She saw no insurmountable problems. "But," I protested, "how can it possibly work?"

I knew that Ned could learn to read words. He had done that

when he was a tiny child. Recently Barbara had been showing him sight-reading cards, and he had done well and had enjoyed it too. But she had been using a fraction of the words the Institutes thought necessary and had presented them at a moderate speed, reviewing constantly. I also knew Ned was able to read some words spontaneously. That had been wonderfully demonstrated shortly after we had moved to Pasadena. I was out driving with Ned when he suddenly shouted out, "Doughnut!" I looked around expecting to see a Winchell's Doughnut Shop nearby, but all I saw was an old auto parts store. Oh, I thought to myself, he sees the tires. I was about to explain that tires look something like doughnuts when he repeated, "Doughnut!" Then I saw it. In faded paint, on the side of the building we were just passing, was the barely legible word "doughnut." But learning two thousand words in a few months was something else. And could he possibly learn anything seeing ten cards in fifteen seconds? Again Barbara's response was completely different from mine. She thought this approach would increase Ned's interest by covering a great deal more territory with a speed that left no room for boredom.

There was to be no testing in the intelligence program. We were never to ask Ned to repeat words or to read aloud or to show us in any way that he was absorbing the material. I liked that. The amount of testing done in school had always struck me as one of the miseries of education. And for hurt kids all that testing must be very threatening. "Testing is just to make teachers feel better," we were told. "It doesn't do anything for the kids." That was an intriguing thought. And there was another important rule. It was to be fun. We were to be cheerful and positive about his intelligence program and about our faith in his ability to learn. The staff even said that we might find that the intelligence program would be so much fun for Ned that reading lessons could be used as rewards during the physical program. This sounded somewhat farfetched to me, but again, Barbara's enthusiasm bore me along. Well, I thought to myself, if she understands the intelligence program so well, she can be in charge of it. I'll take simple creeping and crawling.

Though the week was over, we were told not to make a decision until we had returned home. It would be too easy under the inspiration of the hard-working and dedicated staff and the magic words of Glenn Doman to say yes. We should think carefully about making a commitment to this program. It would be very difficult and demanding. What's more, the Institutes only wanted people who were really going to do it all. They had time to help only a certain number of families, and they didn't want to turn down a family who would be willing to work hard while they wasted time with anyone who wasn't seriously interested. This was understandable. Besides, we needed time to think about the impact this program would have on our lives and about organizing ourselves to do it. I would be going back to work soon. Could Barbara do this alone? What about school? There were so many questions to be answered.

On the plane returning to Los Angeles, we could talk of nothing else. And our conversation betrayed our ambivalence.

"They're crazy! We can't possibly do this."

"These people say so many things we agree with, they seem to be really talking about Ned."

The next minute we were saying, "We're running out of options, anyway. Let's do it!" And then, "How can we? What a staggering lot of work."

"Maybe we could do the program in his home hours and have him continue at Dubnoff. That way we would have some free time."

"Do you think he could brachiate in the park?"

"Where could we put a patterning table?"

Barbara had her notebook out. She was rearranging our lives.

At home we continued wrestling with the decision. We did some experimenting to see how it would go. We rolled up the rugs, and Ned crawled on the bare wood floors. He was perfectly willing, but I could see that he would need a better crawling surface. We tried creeping in the back yard, and again cooperation wasn't a problem. We started the vitamin supplements and diet. I took Ned to the park to see if I could get him to perform on an overhead ladder. Not much success there. Too many distractions. We would have to have our own ladder. We were learning about what we would need and what changes we would have to make if we were really going to do the program.

Ned returned to his former schedule, and we had a conference with Robin, now the principal at Dubnoff, to tell her all we had learned in Philadelphia. She was interested, of course, but rather skeptical, and she didn't see how Dubnoff could really be part of Ned's life while he was on this kind of program.

The more we thought about it, the more it became clear to us that we had to give Ned this chance and that we could not do it in a halfhearted way. Realistically, there would be no way to accomplish so much in the seven hours left after school. Okay! We would do it! We would take Ned out of school, and we would give our all to this therapy. If it didn't work out, we would never regret trying. Meanwhile, Ned continued at Dubnoff while we prepared ourselves to go to work.

As I was concerned about the stipulation that Ned was to stay on his hands and knees, I was eager to get the makings of the restrictive harness described in a drawing I had been given at the Institutes. In the meantime we simply asked Ned to stay on the floor, and he was surprisingly compliant. We kept him interested by having him creep for anything he wanted.

"Can I swing?"

"Yes, creep out the door and all the way to the swing."

Not only was he willing, he seemed to enjoy it.

"Great creeping, Ned!" After a few days I abandoned my harness making.

I knew that we were asking a lot of Ned, and I felt anything he was asked to do, I should be willing to do myself. When he crawled, I would crawl, and when he crept, I would creep. The vinyl I originally bought for a crawling surface was a failure. I replaced it with four two-foot-wide rolls of carpeting. They were thick enough when unrolled on our brick terrace to give a fairly soft surface, although my knees and elbows began to take a beating. It wasn't long before I had to give up crawling; I just couldn't keep up with Ned. I was better at creeping. I had mapped out a large circular track in the back yard, and we crept around the apricot trees, up to the back wall, and down past the avocado. As each day passed, Ned achieved greater and greater distances.

Barbara was making word and phrase cards at a tremendous rate. There were cards spread out across the dining room, and everywhere there were lists. Two thousand words! We alerted friends that we needed their help.

We used a kitchen timer, setting it to ring every seven minutes, and started to work on masking. We wore stopwatches around our necks to time each one-minute masking precisely. The first day we managed only twelve, and we were supposed to do forty!

We had been putting off the start of patterning. Where could we put a patterning table? The work and materials of the program were all over the house, and we wanted to be able to put them away at the end of the day so we could relax and rebuild our strength for tomorrow. Having a fairly normal-looking home was important to us, and the addition of a patterning table, a cumbersome object, presented quite a problem. Our solution was to put an exercise pad on the dining room table, satisfying the needs of the program and preserving our aesthetic standards too. We had also been worrying about how cooperative Ned would be with having us manipulate his body. But now that we had the table problem solved, it was time to begin.

For our third patterner we needed someone Ned loved and trusted, and we wanted to be good at patterning ourselves before we attempted to teach John. We called Harry. Could he come over and help us pattern for the first time? Our efforts were laughably awkward, and we had to remind ourselves that patterning was serious business. Ned was tolerant of our clumsiness as I manipulated his arm and leg on one side, Harry did the same on the other, and Barbara moved his head. Five minutes is really quite a long time, and our arms and backs were tired, but after a few practice tries the patterns began to go fairly smoothly. John was the next to learn the technique, and it wasn't long before we had initiated most of our friends into the mysteries of patterning. It was essential that we be in sync with each other, and we wanted Ned to feel part of things, so we sang and counted as we moved his arms, legs, and head in the pattern of a perfect crawl. "Row, row, row your boat." "One, two, three, four." And we bought an answering machine so that this important part of our work would not be interrupted by the telephone.

So much was changing in our lives. We had only been home a short time, and almost all of our daily activities were different. We called Mary Silberzahn and Dr. Knepflar to discontinue therapies. "But," Mary protested, "Ned would have made wonderful progress if he had done my therapy twelve hours a day." Maybe so, but she hadn't asked us to. No one except the Institutes understood the extent to which we were willing to go to help our child.

On Ned's tenth birthday we had a farewell party for his Dubnoff class. They came to our house for a rollicking day. There was no sadness at leaving Dubnoff. They had done their best for him over a four-year-period, but it was time for a change and for a major effort to see what we could accomplish.

We called Dr. Salley and informed her of our plan to do the Institutes program. She was not at all in accord with our decision. She disagreed with the Institutes approach and felt she could not continue as Ned's physician if we persisted in this therapy. Well, that was that.

There was one more hurdle. The Pasadena Unified School District was still responsible for Ned's education, and we were taking him out of school. One of the psychologists visited us and discussed our plans; wonder of wonders, she was wholly supportive. She suggested that the school district could provide a home teacher to help out. "Of course," she said, "I will have to find you someone who will be positive and interested in this kind of program." Well, this was an unexpected bonus!

Our friends were rallying around. Harry became a regular patterner. Aneta took pictures and contributed her beautiful lettering. Kay and Bernie brought food. Everyone left taking marking pens and cards with them for the manufacture of intelligence materials. Those who couldn't come to our house worked on lists at home. They all were excited for us that we had something new to do for Ned.

Dianne, one of the aides from Ned's Dubnoff classroom, was available and willing to work with us. She had been particularly interested in Ned. She had taught him to roller-skate, had taken him home for overnights and out to the movies. She had brought her little nephew over as a playmate. Now she was joining our team.

With the arrival of the brachiation ladder we had ordered, we finally had all the parts of the program in place. In most cases we were only accomplishing a tiny portion of what we needed to do to reach our goals, but at least it was a beginning. Barbara designed a record-keeping chart, a daily log with spaces to record every detail of our program. We kept it on a clipboard, and each evening as we finished our daily entries, we would see progress toward those seemingly impossible goals.

Almost immediately we began to see small changes in Ned. He was beginning to use his index finger to scratch himself instead of his former full-hand scratching. His speech began to sound clearer, especially final sounds: "Yogur*t*." He had stopped rocking in his bed. He still rocked his head from side to side but wasn't so detached while doing it. Every day he seemed more responsive. Was it possible that all these things were happening? Was the program really responsible, or was it just due to all the individual attention he was getting? Or was it going to happen anyway? The Institutes staff were fond of saying, with a certain degree of irony, "This is the place where all the things happen that were going to happen anyway."

Ned had his one hour a day when he could be on his feet, running and walking and roller-skating, and we tried to make that time a reward for all the hard work he was doing. We had been on the program only two weeks when we took a brisk walk in the Arroyo and Ned did absolutely *no* leaf tearing. This had to be a miracle. He seemed to have awakened from a dream. His walk had a spring to it we had never seen. His shoulders were held in a more relaxed way. These little signs of normalcy were exciting to us. Only last fall we had been told that he had gone as far as he could go!

As the hot weather came on, we moved the creeping and crawling track into the garage, taking turns monitoring the work. One afternoon as Ned valiantly circled the garage and driveway, Barbara stood next to the washing machine lettering more cards for his intelligence program and urging Ned on. "Good creeping. You are great, Ned!" With each lap she read him a lesson. As she flashed the card "sweat" at him, she misread it as "sweet."

"That's 'sweat,' " Ned corrected her. "Sweat" was a new word for him, but "sweater" had been in his lessons last week.

There were a lot of hot days that summer, and sometimes after hurrying to get the program done, the four of us would drive to the ocean for a picnic supper. Ned would stay on all fours, but at the beach it hardly showed; lots of kids were creeping about, playing in the sand.

The program was enormously absorbing. Barbara and I were full of thinking about it, talking about it, and doing it, and John was excited about it with us. Although he was often too involved in his own activities to help much with Ned's program, he continued to pattern with us. He certainly seemed to be accepting of all the attention we were giving his brother. I thought that John probably felt as we did, that it was better to be doing something rather than sitting by waiting for the professionals to work their wonders on Ned. We had all felt so helpless for so long.

John was playing Little League baseball with great success. One of us would always go to his game, and the other would bring Ned over for his "up" hour to see John play.

Pasadena, California
June 28, 1978

Howdy Grammy,

I hope you're feeling better soon. Everyone around here is doing just fine. Well, my Little League season has ended and our team did pretty well, but we didn't make the play-offs. I hit 295 and was nominated most valuable infielder on the team.

I'll be going to a camp on Catalina Island for two weeks this summer and a soccer camp at my school for five days.

Dad and I are going to the Dodger game tonight.

XXXOOO
Love, John

PS Mother wanted me to send you my report card which I am very proud of. Be SURE to send back my report card.

When the "season" was over, the usual team party was held, and we worked diligently to complete Ned's program early so that we could all attend. Ned was great from the moment we arrived. He was very interested in watching the boys play in the pool. First he stood apart, observing carefully. Then he got in the pool too and began to swim underwater, tread water, swim on his back. All the while, Ned was aware of the kids, laughing at their antics. When one of the mothers said good-bye to Ned, he piped up, "Good-bye, Linda." He had picked up her name! Everyone commented on the progress he had made. It was a landmark day. People who had seen Ned through the years at John's games were able to perceive the changes we were seeing. We definitely had hope now, there was no denying it.

On the Fourth of July we all went to a party at the Harps. Dr. Harp had seen something of Ned following our dismal experience at NPI when Ned was having his bladder control problems, and we were eager to see if he noticed the change. Ned was not at his very best that day, yet Grady commented that he saw "great improvement. He's showing so much affection, attention, language." We were terribly pleased. Grady is an excellent observer and very direct. His confirmation of our views of Ned's progress was important to us.

Barbara and I could hardly wait the three weeks until we returned to Philadelphia. We were eager to show off our new Ned to the staff at the Institutes. They would understand how much hard work had gone into his improvement.

Pasadena, California
July 20, 1978

Dear Grammy,

Thank you very much for the stamps. I will enjoy them very much. Our All-Star team won its first game yesterday 6–5. If we win our next game Saturday I won't be able to go to Philly for I will have obligations to play.

OOOXXX
Love, John Christopher

PS I went to the doctor the other day for my physical and he said I grew three-and-a-half inches last year!

John's All-Star team did win that next game, and as he put it, he had obligations. We were eager to show John the Institutes; he was a part of all that was happening. But baseball came first for him and he couldn't go. What's more, the "M*A*S*H" season had begun, so I couldn't be in Philadelphia myself until the end of our appointment week there. So Barbara had all the excitement of returning for reevaluation and sharing with the staff what had gone on during two and a half months of program. She had so much to tell. Everything was better. There was the leaf-tearing miracle and his talking. He had begun to take an interest in what was going on outside and would look out his bedroom window, commenting on the passing scene. "There's Patsy out there." "There's a white car out there." "The baby's crying out there." One day Ned had shown great concern for Barbara when she stubbed her toe. This was very new. He had always been oblivious to our feelings, our pains.

When I arrived in Philadelphia, Barbara couldn't wait to fill me in. Ned had done fabulously well on his reevaluation. This time when he was asked to identify objects in a bag by touch, he got them all right. We had not taught the task; we had just done the program, and Ned had grown so much in tactile awareness that he could now perform with 100 percent accuracy. The Institutes staff had tested Ned's reading, and he had identified all the words he had been asked by handing over the appropriate card. Ned's respiration had improved, and everyone had been impressed with his work on the ladder. That made me smile. I knew he would wow them. His hands, now as tough as little paws, were looked at admiringly. To them callused knees and tough hands were beautiful. And to us too, by now.

Ned wasn't the only one in our kumi who had made progress. Kids who hadn't been able to move at all when we first met them were inching their way across the padded floor; a paralyzed girl had begun to move one of her hands; all the kids were demonstrating that they had learned their reading words. Once more parents shared their experiences and compared their new programs, groaning and laughing at the impossible demands of this remarkable place we had come to know only two and a half months earlier.

We should have known! We had done such a great job and Ned had made so much progress that our new program was even harder than the last! Now Ned was going to crawl one half-mile daily with an end goal of accomplishing this in one hour, non-stop. And he was going to creep two miles! He was also going to do sprint creeping and crawling. His brachiation was increased, he had more maskings, and he had more, much more intelligence program. And there was a new element too. He was going to run. Run? Ned? Ned had always liked to dash about, but he would only run a few yards and then begin to jump up and down in place. We had never thought him capable of endurance running at a track. Now he had a goal of running three miles in thirty minutes, plus twenty forty-yard sprints daily.

By this time we were a dedicated Institutes family. We went back home, took a deep breath, and began our new program. Barbara designed a new record-keeping chart for the clipboard, and Ned plunged right in.

Three months earlier, if it had been suggested to me that Ned could do sustained running, I would simply have said, "Well, maybe someday. I know what running is, I know what it looks like. Ned won't look like that. He won't really be running." How foolish! When we first encountered Glenn Doman and his philosophy, I thought in terms of success and failure. Then I heard him tell a very simple story. To give a little brain-injured girl the experience of being upright, the Institutes suggested to her family that she should hang from a horizontal bar for one minute. "She can never do that," said her parents, "but we will give it a try." So they put little Suzie's hands on the bar and after two seconds, she dropped off. Her parents could have said, "Too bad, Suzie, you failed," or they could have said, "Nice try, but you just can't do it." But what they learned to say and what every Institutes family learns to say is, "Suzie, you are wonderful! You are the greatest little kid in all the world. You hung on for two seconds and that was fantastic." We were beginning to conceive of Ned's life and his daily challenges only in terms of success.

So off we went to the track, dressed in our new running shorts and shoes. Though our goal was a three-mile, non-stop run, we were to start by running a half mile, then walking a quarter mile, then running another half mile. And when we started that morning with what was to be Ned's first half mile, his run was strange looking indeed, a sort of shuffle. But I accepted it without question. I lavished praise. I sang, "One-two, one-two," and, "Good-job-run-ning," as we made our way along the track. For the entire half mile I kept my feet in step with his. During the walk I kept on counting so he would know it was all part of the same task. And he did it. "You are great, Ned," I shouted. And he was.

In a shorter time than I could have believed possible, Ned's running style began to look like real running. I continued to run alongside him, counting out the paces. Barbara joined us, but Ned was soon lapping her. We were at the track each evening, Ned, Barbara, Pepper, and I. John thought running was "boring" and usually declined to join us. But we weren't bored and Ned wasn't bored and Pepper was delighted with this unexpected behavior on our part.

Ned's program had changed in other ways. He could now be on his feet when he wasn't creeping or crawling. He had "basic vision" therapy to improve his light reflexes. Six times a day one of us would go into the front hall closet with him for one minute and turn on and off a five-hundred-watt bulb (one second on, five seconds off).

There was a new kind of intelligence program. Ned was to be presented with "bits of information," sophisticated, large, and beautiful flash cards, covering a wide array of subjects. We were given very specific instructions on how to make these "bits" and how they were to be organized. Bits were to be made of clear, discrete pictures mounted on eleven-inch-square cards with precise labels lettered on the back: California Black Bear, Indian Paintbrush, Geronimo. The pictures, cut from magazines, books, and posters, were to be accurate representations, photographs rather than drawings. They were to be presented in categories: mammals of North America, wild flowers of the Sierra Nevada, American Indians. Again the speed of presentation was to be as rapid as possible, fifteen seconds to show a group of ten bits. Ten groups of bits were to be presented three times a day for five days and then retired.

As part of this new intelligence program, Ned was going to have "homemade books," a new one every five days. These were short, simple books that Barbara would compose and letter on eleven-inch-square cards, illustrated with pictures placed between each one-sentence page.

Audubon

John James Audubon was a naturalist.
He traveled around the United States and made paintings of the birds he saw.
His paintings were very careful and showed just what the birds looked like.
Audubon was born in 1785 and died in 1851.

Ned was to see homemade books three times a day, too. He continued to have new words and sentences, and he had a math program. I began to be very grateful that Barbara was an artist. Her two years of lettering classes were really paying off! She threw herself into the work. These new lessons covered all kinds of subjects: science, history and art, symbols and arcane alphabets, and botany and biology. Again, we called on our friends. Barbara was going to be producing thousands and thousands of cards, and we needed their help. Ned loved the new materials. His intelligence lessons became his favorite reward throughout the day. "Look at cards! Can I look at cards?" he would say.

Our second reevaluation was in October. John was able to go with us this time. He attended some of the lectures and met the other siblings of kids on the program, normal brothers and sisters who could run about, play games, laugh and talk, and make instant friends. By this time John had been living in the midst of Ned's Institutes program for six months and had put in many hours of patterning himself. He was proud of Ned's progress and was impressed that there were so many families working just as hard as we did. But his real interest that October was the baseball playoffs in which the Dodgers were facing the Phillies.

Just as on the previous visit, we had brought all of our statistics. The Institutes wanted exact information about every aspect of our program: exactly how many yards Ned had crept, crawled, and brachiated; the number of maskings and patternings; our log on Ned's running. We had filled out a diet sheet specifying exactly what Ned had eaten at every meal and for snacks for the week before returning. We knew the exact number of bits of information, reading words, sentences, homemade books, and math cards Ned had seen.

Not surprisingly, we all passed with flying colors. Ned had done a fantastic job. His calluses were beautiful. His running had become a new source of pride, and he had achieved all his goals. New therapies were added as the staff analyzed Ned's growth: a program of rolling, somersaulting, and vertical spinning; a sensory stimulation program to help Ned overcome his lack of appropriate response in taste, smell, sound, and touch. Adjustments were made in the intelligence program: size of lettering, length of sentences, complexity of material.

Each time we returned to the Institutes, we were challenged almost beyond our imagination. But also on each revisit, we were asked a few simple questions: "What is the worst thing that has happened since we last saw you?" "What is the best thing?" "How do you rate Ned's improvement?" "Has it been worth the effort?" And each time our answer to the last question was an unqualified yes! We were always asked what we thought the essential problem was. And as we worked with Ned through months and months of program, we became more aware that his problem was one of neurological organization, that he took in a great deal of information but that the information he took in was not well enough organized within his brain to be useful to him. That, we began to see, was why Ned could learn so well through the Institutes intelligence program. Everything was organized for him, and he could then use much, much more of the information.

Back at Twentieth Century Fox, we began our seventh season, and I couldn't help telling my "M*A*S*H" colleagues about the program. Everyone on the show knew Ned, of course; I talked about him often, and they had seen him over the years at the annual Christmas parties, diving into the buffet with enthusiasm, covering his ears against the loud music, and on one memorable occasion emptying the water cooler. I was eager to share my excitement about Ned's progress, and I couldn't help boasting about all the creeping and running I had been doing myself. "We thought you seemed a lot smarter this year," Alan Alda mused. "This explains it."

Harry came to visit me on the set and I took him around, showing him my dressing room in one of the oldest buildings on one of the oldest lots in Hollywood. We had lunch in the commissary and then returned to stage 9. I was called to the phone, and it was Barbara.

"Does Harry have a teaching job yet?"

"No. It's a bad year for teachers."

"Well, I've had a sudden inspiration," she said. "Do you think we could hire Harry to help us with the program? Dianne isn't going to be available as many hours."

I put it to him gently. "Don't say anything, Harry. Don't say a word. You're going to work with us on the program. Don't worry, you'll love it. And we go running every evening. You'll be in great shape in no time."

And so Harry came to work for us, helping to manufacture masses of intelligence materials, working with Ned, and keeping us all cheerful. As I predicted, he was in great shape in no time. "If I'd started earlier in life, I think I could have been an athlete," he gasped, as we both kept pace with Ned at the track.

One thing was becoming a problem. Our wonderful little house was just that, wonderful but little. We now had a large "family." There were people and materials all over the house all the time, and we absolutely had to have more space.

Pasadena, California
December 23, 1978

Dear Grandpa Jim,
Happy Birthday! Well as you must have heard, we are going to

be moving. Our new house is very nice and I can't wait. But we
don't move in until March.

School is going just fine and I can't wait until Christmas. Say
hello to Grandma for me and I hope you two will come out and see
the house soon.

Love, John

We had found a big, old Craftsman house right in the
neighborhood. We loved the area so much that we hadn't
considered moving out of it. We made sure that Ned knew he
was going with us this time, and we didn't expect a problem;
we were only moving a few blocks away. We managed to do
the program all the time we were packing and cleaning, and the
move was accomplished on schedule in early March. But the
change wasn't as easy for Ned as we had confidently hoped.
He cried for weeks: "Can I go home?" "Can I go home?" But
even through his tears he crept and crawled and brachiated
and ran.

The new house had a rather odd floor plan: kitchen, dining
room, laundry, and storage room on the lower floor and living
room and bedrooms upstairs. This meant all of our work was
done downstairs. We manufactured materials in the large
storeroom; the creeping and crawling track was laid out in the
long, narrow hallway; and when we went upstairs for the
evening, we could leave it all behind us. It was a perfect
arrangement for us and for the program.

Before we knew it, we were back at the Institutes for
reevaluation. On this revisit we were surprised with a new
directive. We were to go off the program for a month and see
how Ned would do. We could use the time to do all those
things we hadn't had a chance to do for the past year. We could
even travel.

Auckland, New Zealand
April 15, 1979

Dear Grandma and Grandpa Jim,
I like N.Z. a lot and I especially enjoyed seeing Rugby which is

a game they play here which is similar to football. I also enjoyed seeing the thermal geysers and bubbling mud in Rotorua. I think that Ned is enjoying our trip also. Ned says [Ned's writing inserted] HI. And so do Mom and Dad. Dad is working on a commercial right now. Hope to see you soon.

Love and OOOXXX,
John

Ned did well on our travels, running on the beautiful beaches, eating countless shrimp cocktails in restaurants, enjoying the hotels and plane trips and ferries and long drives through the mountainous landscape. By the time we returned to Pasadena, he was willing to call the new house "home." He settled into his new room, the old sleeping porch of the house, and we celebrated his eleventh birthday by returning to the hard work of the program.

We were now in a routine. It was back to Philadelphia every six months, the weeks spent there all structured the same way. The program kept getting harder, Ned kept getting better, and we were loving it and feeling a great sense of achievement. Between the challenges of the program and my shooting schedule, we managed to squeeze in some major improvements to the garden, and by fall we began restoring the house.

Pasadena, California
October 20, 1979

Dear Grandma,

Happy birthday!! How are you? We're all fine. We are having the dining room stripped so it will have wooden walls but still a white ceiling. School is going fairly well and I'm having a good time. Good luck with your surgery in Boston. Ned is doing very well on his program so far and he's running quite a bit now, about 3½ miles a day cross-country.

So far our football team has done very well and our record is four wins and no losses. But we have our biggest game tomorrow against Mayfield.

I've been noticing that gold is very much on the rise so I've been

thinking of selling my two shares of AT&T and investing in gold.
But this is a bad time to sell my stock because it is near an all-time
low. But also I figure the nation's economy isn't going to get too
much better real soon and that now is as good a time as any.

Love, John
XXXOOO

We crowded as much as possible into our lives during the
holidays that year: Thanksgiving at Leona's, a two-day trip to
Yosemite, my parents and niece for a Christmas visit, fourteen
people for Christmas dinner, forty for the Rose Parade. We
were so exhilarated by the success of the program, so proud of
Ned, so delighted with John, so content in our new home, so
thankful for the blessings of our existence, and we sailed into
1980 with unbeatable energy and optimism and some exciting
plans.

Pasadena, California
February 6, 1980

Dear Mother:
Just a note while I have a chance. We are having glorious
weather. I wish you were here to see the clear blue sky, bask in the
sun, and see my flowers. All the camellias are in bloom, lots of
primroses, daffodils, and azaleas too. The acacia is just starting,
and in my flower bed I have poppies and calendulas flowering.
Also forsythia, pansies. Really something!
Our Italian trip is all planned, our deposits paid, and we are
quite excited! I am reading heavily and want to thank you for the
guidebooks on Florence and Rome. They are excellent and have so
much detail. I think it is a good idea to know what is there so we
can narrow down what we try to see. It's obvious that we can't go
to every church or museum. Even without the kids that would be
difficult and with them IMPOSSIBLE. We are going to have fun
and visit Italy and see what we can of the historical places.
Now that "M*A*S*H" is through filming, we are getting
some things done around here. We have sorted out all of our
books. Next I am tackling the clothes and storage areas. We aren't

doing any furnishing at the moment as we are resting that part of our brains!

Harry will take care of our house and Pepper while we are away.

Love and kisses, B.

PS Love to Jim.

There was a note on the back in Ned's writing:

Hi, Grammy. Love, Ned.

We had the program well in hand. Ned was progressing and happy. And next time we returned to the Institutes, we would keep going in the same direction. East to Italy!

CHAPTER 7

Molto Bene, Grazie

*B*uon giorno, Ned."
"*Buon giorno, Mamma.*"

It was our first morning in Italy, and I awakened Ned in our Rome hotel. Eager to see what we had come to see, we all dressed quickly and went out into the bracing spring air. The four of us walked across the city to the Vatican and stood in the square with the multitudes as the Easter Mass rolled out over us in language after language. Ned looked about him with an air of wonder.

"Do you know where we are, Ned?" I asked.

"St. Peter's in the Vatican."

"That's right, Ned. Tell me who designed the dome."

"Michelangelo."

"Absolutely correct. You are really great, Ned. Tell me who designed the colonnade."

"Bernini."

"Fantastic!"

Bill and I had spent the last three months preparing Ned and ourselves for our Italian trip. We had used the Institutes intelligence materials to teach him something of the history of each of the cities we were going to visit; to teach the important periods of art history in Italy; to teach the art itself, particularly the specific great works we were going to see; to teach some of the myths—Romulus and Remus, Scylla and Charybdis; and to teach a few words of Italian—polite phrases and favorite foods.

Bits of information used in the intelligence program were

organized into sets and labeled with their category names. Our categories were based on whatever good pictures we could lay our hands on. With Italy in our future we had constant inspiration for new categories: paintings in the Borghese Gallery or Etruscan sculpture or Greek temples in Sicily. Travel brochures, magazines, and art books were a rich source of illustrations. Guidebooks and encyclopedias provided subject matter for homemade books. When planning a trip we usually read a great deal to prepare ourselves for what we were going to see. Now we could bring Ned into that preparation, and it was exciting to organize it the way we had been taught at the Institutes. Ned was almost twelve, and his progress over the last two years allowed me to use age-appropriate subject matter and sophisticated language in making his materials. Anything that I could in any way associate with our travels I immediately made into a book—Juliet's balcony speech or a biography of Julius Caesar or the history of Siena or a specific period of art history, such as the Byzantines in Italy or . . .

Romanesque

The architecture and decoration of the early Middle Ages is called Romanesque.
[picture of the Monreale Cloister]

In the 11th, 12th, and 13th centuries, great churches were built in this style.
[picture of the cathedral at Palermo]

They had exterior arcades, detached bell towers, and elaborately carved facades.
[picture of Assisi]

The Church of St. Zeno is one of Italy's finest Romanesque churches. It is in Verona. The doors of the church are a great work of art in themselves.
[picture of the doors of St. Zeno]

The Basilica of St. Francis in Assisi is another great Romanesque building.

[picture of the Basilica of St. Francis]

The mosaics of the dome of the Baptistry in Florence are great examples of Romanesque decoration.

[picture of the mosaics in the Baptistry]

In Sicily the decor of the Palatine Chapel in Palermo and the Abbey at Monreale are dazzling examples of Romanesque mosaic decoration.

[picture of mosaics in Monreale]

Perhaps the most famous examples in the world of this period are the Baptistry and Leaning Tower of Pisa.

[picture of the Cathedral, Baptistry, and Leaning Tower]

The panels of the doors of the cathedral in Pisa by Bonnano Pisano are great bronze Romanesque works.

[picture of the doors]

We knew Ned would enjoy these lessons. We had found out early in our work with him that he particularly liked looking at art. And Italy is so full of art. We also realized that museum after museum might be too taxing for us. We decided in advance which objects and paintings we were going to look at in each museum. We made sure that Ned had seen a photograph of each of these works of art; that he had heard facts about the art, the buildings, the museums; and that he knew which city to expect to see them in. We also presented a lesson on how to behave in museums, just in case.

We returned to the Vatican on a rainy day to visit the museums. ("The Vatican contains some of the greatest works of art in the world.") Ned managed to stand patiently in line for over an hour. We walked through the Egyptian and Pio-Clementino museums and the Raphael rooms ("Raphael's rooms painted for Pope Julius II are in the Vatican; they are his masterpiece") to the Sistine Chapel ("Michelangelo painted the ceiling of the Sistine Chapel"), where we were so enchanted at seeing Ned stare at the ceiling, moving his gaze to each section of familiar painting, that we didn't notice when my pocket was picked. We retraced our steps to look at the works we had singled out to teach Ned. ("The Vatican art collection includes some of the greatest ancient sculpture including the *Apollo Belvedere* and the *Laocoön*.") He stared at the *Laocoön* in obvious recognition and the *Apollo Belvedere* and the *Venus of Cnidus* and the *Torso of the Belvedere*. Then we climbed Michelangelo's dome and looked out over the Eternal City.

Rome
April 11, 1980

Dear Grandma and Grandpa Jim,
We are having a very good time in Italy. Thank you very much for the money as I am able to use it here very easily. I cannot seem to decide what I have liked best because we've seen so much. But I did really like St. Peter's.

OOOXXX
Love, John

John had been less excited about traveling to Italy than we had hoped and in fact had announced that he didn't want to go to Italy at all; he preferred France—anything but Italy. This was no doubt attributable to the fact that he had been a reluctant Latin student for the past two years. But now that we were actually here, he was enjoying Italy greatly, managing to ignore the schoolbooks he had brought along on the trip. He discovered that great comforter of American travelers in Europe, the *Herald Tribune*, which carried the baseball scores from home. Finding the newsstand and managing the purchase of the paper or going out to buy yogurt for Ned, Berlitz phrase book in hand, became his routine. He was delighted, of course, that with his dark hair and brown eyes he was taken for Italian wherever we went. The waiters would turn to him immediately, having spotted the rest of us as obvious tourists.

We made some mistakes. Italy is famous for its ice cream and the Piazza Navona, one of Rome's most elegant squares ("The Piazza Navona was the scene of chariot races in ancient times"), has some of the best of that best of ice creams. For the past two years we had been strictly observing the Institutes guidelines on nutrition, but here we were in Rome. We would let Ned have some Italian ice cream. We sat in an outdoor café and ordered. When it arrived, we were each presented with ten scoops, all different flavors. Ned's eyes grew huge. This couldn't be for him. He dove in, and I didn't have the heart to say, "That's enough, Ned." He ate every bite. We all did. But as we walked back to our hotel, Ned became wild. He ran along the street laughing, heedless of the cars. We raced back to the hotel and made it to the room without anything awful happening, but just barely. Safe in our room we sat back to watch the results of our carelessness. Ned was in a highly excitable state and did not calm down until noon of the following day. We wouldn't make that mistake again.

As we settled into the life of being tourists, Ned became more and more comfortable.

"*Buon giorno,*" said the concierge.

"*Buon giorno,*" answered Ned.

"*Come stai?*"

"*Molto bene, grazie.*"

He loved the hotel and, as always, the restaurants. He ordered, "*Fragole.*" It was spring, after all, and Italian strawberries were just as good as the ice cream any day. And after sampling the wine that was routinely placed in front of the children in Italian restaurants, Ned learned to order his usual milk. "*Latte, per favore.*"

Having learned a few things in Rome, we continued our tour. We walked the streets of Pompeii, missing some of the more important sights because Bill, consulting his guidebook and discoursing on the life of an actor in ancient times, insisted on seeing every one of the theaters.

After driving south along the coast, we crossed the Strait of

Messina, recalling the myths of Odysseus and Scylla and Charybdis. We drove through Sicily on winding country roads, through mountains and blooming fields of daisies, thistles, poppies, and many unfamiliar flowers of red, yellow, blue, purple, and pink. In Agrigento and Selinunte the boys romped through ruined temples of a beauty beyond imagination. We ferried to Naples and drove north through the hill towns, stopping to see each scheduled piece of art, and climbed the terrifying Tower of Pisa. (The Leaning Tower of "Pizza," as Ned and probably thousands of other American kids called it.)

Florence
April 20, 1980

Dear Mother:
We passed through Pisa on our way to Florence. The leaning tower is wonderful. I felt askew myself when I came down. We traveled through lovely countryside. Florence is more frantic than I thought it would be, but we have seen some wonderful art. David alone would be worth the trip. And we loved the convent of San Marco. Some rain today but spirits undampened.

Love, B.

We had all stood amazed in front of the *David.* John was fascinated by the sculpting of the hands. Ned greeted an old friend, "David!"

We drove through the Apennines, picnicking along the side of the road, and through the Pineta that Byron loved so much ("Lord Byron, the great English poet, lived in Italy") to Ravenna. In Ravenna John found what he had been looking for. He had heard us talking about Palladian arcades, but to him, a contemporary American teenager, an arcade was a place for electronic games. Ravenna, the city of the great Byzantine mosaics ("Ravenna's Mausoleum of Galla Placidia is one of the oldest examples of early Christian architecture"), had a video arcade! While John played Italian PacMan, Ned and Bill and I walked around on the street. Ned spied some children chasing each other along the curb side. He ran to them and gleefully joined in the chase. He began to circle a pole, laughing with delight. The kids tried to talk to him in their rapid Italian, and he just laughed, circling the pole. It took some time to cross the language barrier, but as I stood watching, my heart swelling with pride at how well Ned was doing, one of the kids gave him a knowing glance. He turned to the others. *"Scempio,"* he said with a shrug. They all looked at Ned who was still smiling and running about, and they ran off. He was doing very well but he still couldn't join the gang. Not in Italy, not anywhere.

In Verona ("In Verona the house in which Juliet is said to have lived still stands") we stood in the courtyard under Juliet's balcony, and Ned, with a bit of motherly prompting, recited Juliet's famous soliloquy. Did the other tourists who smiled in amazement at him know that this was a "handicapped" boy? That he was *"scempio"*? ("What's in a name? A rose by any other name would smell as sweet.") We went to markets and ate in street cafés and walked everywhere. We ended our travels gliding along the canals of Venice.

Our trip could not have gone better. At the very last minute there was a hitch in Alitalia scheduling, and we were delayed eight hours, but no matter. We were safely on the plane, and my mother and Jim, willing to drive all the way down from Glastonbury to help us pass the hours between flights, would be waiting for us at Kennedy, eager to hear about our travels.

We landed and started the arduous slog through customs, and Ned began to get restless. Leaving Bill and John with the bags, I took Ned to the upper lobby and tried to amuse him, but he squirmed away from me and climbed onto a large glass display platform. I couldn't allow that and tried to persuade him to get down. Finally I reached up and lifted him down. Infuriated, he suddenly lit into me, crying loudly, grabbing and pinching my breasts. Oh, God! What's happening? What is the matter? I asked myself desperately. Ned had never behaved like this before. He had become a little wild animal. Could I possibly get him under control? I knew he was tired—we all were; we had been traveling for twenty-four hours since leaving our Venice hotel room. But what was I going to do? In a tiny unoccupied corner of my mind I saw what we must look like, a tall woman in a bright blue dress and a wiry, blond boy evidently at odds about something. As I struggled with Ned in a kind of ballet-wrestle, I couldn't help being grateful that I had decided to wear a new dress to travel in. After all, I thought, every eye in the airport must be on us. A man asked if he could help, but I was afraid a stranger might frighten Ned and make things worse. John appeared and I said, "Get Dad."

"I can't. He's busy in customs."

"Get him anyway!"

I spotted my mother on the other side of the barrier. She was aware of my plight, but she couldn't come to my aid because we hadn't cleared customs yet.

Finally an airline worker came up to me. "Would you like me to show you to a place where you can be more private?" I certainly would! She took us behind the scenes, unfortunately seating us next to huge, hot coffee urns. My mother magically appeared at my side while Jim posted himself to spot Bill and direct him to us. Ned was fiercer than ever, and now I was afraid he might burn himself on the coffee, but at least we weren't on display. Finally Bill arrived. He took Ned on his lap, calming him as only he could do, and slowly the crisis abated. My poor mother. She found it hard to believe that the trip had really been a triumph, that Ned had been in public for three weeks straight, standing in line for museums, ordering in restaurants, being quiet in churches, playing with John in parks, aware and interested and altogether our new Ned. Once it was over, we weren't too concerned about Ned's blow-up; we were confident that this was just an isolated episode. With Ned relaxed again, we finally had a chance to visit as we waited for the plane that was to take us back to Los Angeles.

Harry met us at the airport.

"How was it?"

"Absolutely great! Italy is so beautiful."

"I know that, but how about Ned?"

"He was terrific. All that preparation really paid off. And our new program is going to be a big change. You'll never believe it, Harry, but *I* am not to do any work!"

"What do you mean?" he asked suspiciously.

"I'm on a 'mother's honeymoon.'"

On our visit to the Institutes just before leaving for Italy, we had been told that I was to take time off to be just a mother. I was not to be involved in organizing, directing, or running the work. I could play with Ned, take him on outings, but I was to keep hands off the program. It would also be a time to see how well Ned would fare without my constant attention. I could hardly believe it—the whole summer off. Meanwhile with Harry's help and with Bill's free time devoted to the program, Ned would continue to have a pretty full day. We were to use this period to expand Ned's life as much as possible.

Ned's cross-country run was now up to five miles every day. I had long since dropped out of the running; cross-country left me too far behind. Now, with the encouragement of the Institutes to give Ned new experiences, we signed him up for a Perrier 10K race in Beverly Hills. Ned, Bill, and John ran, and Ned crossed the finish line in an hour and twelve minutes, beating 147 other finishers. He would have done better if he had been able to start when everyone else did. But when the gun went off, he was so stunned that he could do nothing. Amid the chaos, as thousands of joggers rushed past him, he stood stock still with his hands over his ears; in seconds he was alone with Bill at the starting line. Bill, unruffled, began the even counting Ned was so used to, "One-two, one-two, one-two." Slowly they moved off at a steady jog. With Bill's quiet urging, Ned began to pick up the pace and finally was passing runner after runner. They entered another 10K at the beach, and again Ned finished and finished well. We were excited about Ned's running ability. Here was something he could do better than many other twelve-year-olds. All in all, he was doing splendidly. The episode at the airport was just a bad dream.

Pasadena, California
June 9, 1980

Dear Grandma,

How are you? We are all fine. I hope your eye operation went well. I've been very busy this last couple of weeks with my final exams and our project which we had to do to graduate. Thank you very much for the record which you sent me for the 29th. I am really enjoying it. I'm glad school is over and am looking forward to doing nothing for a while.

Ned, I think, is doing a lot better since you saw him as he has not blown up at all since then. I think it was a result of not doing the program for so long and he seems to be improving rapidly.

Well, say "Hi" to Grandpa and get well.

OOOXXX
Love, John

Pasadena, California
June 23, 1980

Hi Mother:

The sports season goes on and on. John's team won the league championship, as I told you on the phone. This takes him up through July 12, unless they win, in which case it could continue. He was also selected for the All-Star Team. That goes on until July 24. Unless they win! In which case it could continue! I think I'll root for the other team. He keeps himself busy between triumphs playing golf and tennis. We're busy getting organized but we'll never make it by the time "M*A*S*H" begins shooting.

Love and kisses,
Barbara

From the very beginning the Institutes had provided each family with an advocate, someone to serve as a communication link between the family and the rest of the staff: "This family really can't work in forty creeping and forty crawling sprints along with everything else." Someone to send an occasional letter of encouragement: "Ned, we think you are great!" Someone to prompt families to send in their reports.

Pasadena, California
August 10, 1980

Mrs. Katie Doman
The Institutes for the Achievement of Human Potential
8801 Stenton Avenue
Philadelphia, Pennsylvania

Dear Mrs. Doman:
I have just received your letter inquiring about our interim report. When we were last at the Institutes in April, we were not given an interim report form. I assumed this was because we were assigned a "mother's honeymoon" to last a minimum of three months. It has been a wonderful, restful, and productive period.

In lieu of an official interim report I will outline Ned's activities for this period.

We started with a vacation in Italy. It was incredible and heartening to see how much Ned was able to recall of his intelligence program. He knew architects, artists, places, paintings, and buildings. He could quote Shakespeare (Juliet's balcony speech) and speak a few words of Italian. When he was not able to verbalize his knowledge, it was obvious from the look on his face that he knew what he was seeing. His behavior was excellent and consistently appropriate. We mistakenly bought him some delicious Italian ice ceam one day, and he had a severe hyperactive reaction to it. He also had a tantrum in J. F. K. Airport on our return, but it had been a very trying day and we had been traveling almost twenty-four hours at that point.

After we returned home, Ned went back to work and achieved roughly 100 percent of his physical program. As I was not involved, the work was done in a more informal way than usual. This schedule prevailed through most of June.

As Bill's busy season has come on, Ned has achieved considerably less of his program. However, except on very hot or smoggy days, he has done his five-mile run, and he continues to brachiate as a favorite activity.

Throughout these months Ned has had a chance to do many things not encompassed in his usual routine. He has done very well with swimming and has done more household chores. He has taken more responsibility with food and has helped with yard work.

Most exciting of all, I have read Ned some library books and have found that he is able to make inferences from written material. For example, I read him a book about lions and tigers. On the last page was a picture of a lion with a large joint of meat. I asked Ned what the lion was eating, and he answered, "He killed an animal." This sentence did not appear in the text although there was a description of how lions hunt. I have taken the Institutes' suggestion of asking Ned a question and allowing a very long time for the answer. This works well, and Ned has surprised me daily.

The way Ned plays and initiates play has changed dramatically during this time. He has been playing with a baseball and bat with his brother; he has explored all the possibilities of an inflatable raft in our neighbor's pool; he tosses a ball and swims to it; he is learning to dive; he wants to interact in a playful way; he reaches out to tickle us, etc., etc.

However much we have all enjoyed this relaxed period, we know it has been possible only because of the progress Ned has made through his program and therefore we must get back to work.

One of the questions I asked Ned one day was "Where would you like most to go?" and he answered, "Balboa!" And so as a grand finale of the honeymoon we are going to spend two weeks at Balboa Island, our regular summer vacation spot before we began to work with the Institutes.

We will be ready to go back to work right after Labor Day. It will probably be as difficult to get back on the program as it was to detach myself from the minute to minute involvement in Ned's day. But now that I am finally thoroughly relaxed, I realize how very necessary it was for me to have this time, and I thank you for your wisdom in assigning a "mother's honeymoon."

Ned and Bill join me in sending our best regards to you and Glenn and our other friends at the Institutes. We are looking forward to seeing you soon.

Very truly yours,
Barbara Christopher

Our vacation at Balboa that summer was extraordinary, with Ned joining in the Balboa Island "Yacht Club" activities. This was a recreational program for the children on the island. The dues were a modest one dollar for the season. Bill took Ned there daily where he could jump off the raft following the others, mix with a group of normal kids, and be accepted by them. It was not that they didn't know he was different, but they didn't seem to mind.

Our return to the Institutes that fall brought significant changes. The staff told us that the Civil Code would now be the most important part of Ned's program. Essentially the Civil Code was a token economy with a set of policies to which all family members were required to adhere. Each policy was to be written on a card and shown and explained daily. Ned would have a list of responsibilities, and for accomplishing them he would be paid in poker chips. He could then purchase a privilege as a reward. We had never set great store by rewards, believing that responsibilities were responsibilities and that while it was nice to feel rewarded, it was simply true that many things in life just had to be done anyway. Ned had never been motivated by rewards other than praise and loving attention, and those were built into our life. But the Institutes felt strongly that the Civil Code would help Ned to develop more completely as a functioning member of society. The goal of the Civil Code was "to create a civilized human being who is aware of what is needed and wanted in order to promote his survival and the survival of his family and society."

With the help of staff we developed a detailed breakdown of what our new Civil Code program would be. It reflected our assessment of what we knew Ned was capable of as well as goals we wanted him to strive for.

MIXED BLESSINGS

Our Civil Code

Policies that have been established in our home:
We behave appropriately at all times.
We all share the work of running the house.
We complete Ned's program daily.
We are courteous at home and away from home.
We respect each other's privacy.

Ned's responsibilities:
To do his program.
To make his bed.
To set the table for dinner.
To put his dirty clothes in the basket.
To be responsible for his own bath.
To dress himself within five minutes.
To brush his teeth every morning.
To brush his teeth every evening.
To stay at the dinner table throughout the meal.
To refrain from head shaking for fifteen minutes.
To sit with his feet on the floor while eating.
To greet guests by name.
To wash his own hair.
To eat with fork or spoon.
To cut his meat with a knife.

Ned's privileges:
Play Speak and Spell.
Choose food for supper.
Ten minutes free time.
Eat an apple.
Have crackers and cheese.
Have his back scratched.
Play football with John.
Have a book read to him.
Look at family photo album.
Swim.

Watch TV in the evening.
Roller-skate.
Have a fire in the fireplace.
Trip to the market.
Dinner in a restaurant.
Visit a museum.
Go for a hike.
Visit a park.
Visit the gardens.

We got going on the Civil Code as soon as we arrived home from Philadelphia. Bill, Harry, and I went around with leather bags full of poker chips slung over our shoulders. Ned wore his "code bag" too whenever his program permitted. Our main objective was to see to it that Ned filled his code bag; we were to reward him three hundred times a day! There was a complex system of awards and taxes, with the emphasis on awards. He would receive one poker chip for completing a responsibility. He got an extra chip if he initiated the task himself, three chips if he accomplished the responsibility without being told how to do it, and four chips for promoting the survival of any individual or of the family. (The kettle was boiling, and I failed to notice. Ned said to me, "Answer the tea!" Four chips.) And ten chips for any new responsibility he took on by himself. Ned enjoyed the chips for themselves. We asked him to count them out each evening and to keep them in his code bag. But he didn't understand about spending them, and he often dropped or spilled his chips, not caring enough about them to pick them up.

There were important changes in Ned's intelligence program. We were to provide him with "scripts." (We liked that idea. Bill always enjoyed having scripts around the house!) Ned would learn his script by having it presented to him over a one-week period, and than we would practice the lines. This would give Ned a model on which to build conversation; after all, most of us use scripts all the time: "How are you?" "Fine, thanks." "It's nice to see you." Now Ned would have a script for greeting Stephanie, his home teacher; a script for going to McDonald's and ordering a hamburger and milk; a script for talking to Bill on the telephone; a script for Halloween:

Ned: Trick or treat.
Lee: Oh, I'm so scared!
Ned: Trick or treat, Lee.
Lee: Is that you, Ned? I thought you were a skeleton.
Ned: This is only a costume.
Lee: Here is your treat, Ned.
Ned: Thank you. Happy Halloween.

We had dragooned Lee, our wonderful neighbor, into playing this scene with Ned, and it went fairly well. Ned didn't remember all of his lines, but he did understand that Lee knew hers. Lee had first entered our lives by taking an interest in the program we were doing. She had walked across the street to introduce herself and see what her new neighbors were up to with all that masking and running and brachiation she had seen going on in the yard. She offered the use of her pool whenever Ned could take time out from his work. It was unheated and sometimes pretty chilly, though Ned rarely minded. He came to ask for "cold Lee's pool" at the end of every day.

Another part of Ned's new intelligence program was the dictated letter. I prompted Ned to make up sentences by showing him snapshots, books, and bits, and wrote down his responses. He did quite well with this method, and like any business executive, he signed his own letters.

Hello Grammy: I was a skeleton for Halloween. I scared Lee. I went trick or treat. I got candy. It was fun.

Love, Ned

Dear Grammy: I am reading a story about sly fox and red hen. Sly fox wants to eat red hen. He catches red hen. She gets out of the bag. She puts stones in the bag. She tricks sly fox. This is a great story.

Love, Ned

Dear Grammy: I can make grilled cheese sandwiches. First I cut the cheese. Then I put cheese on bread. Then I put the sandwiches on the grill. I press down with the spatula. Then I turn the sandwich over. It's easy to do. Mommy helps me.

Love, Ned

For the past year the Institutes had allowed us to test Ned. He sat across from me at the round kitchen table each day right after lunch. "Which one is the narwhal?" I asked, showing him two pictures of whales. "That's right, Ned!" I praised, as he selected the correct card. When he had learned this simple selection process, I made the questions more difficult. Showing him two paintings, I asked, "Which one of these was painted in the fifteenth century?" "You are great, Ned. You remember your categories." I showed him a sentence card and asked him to read it to himself. "Which one of these cards is described by the fact you just read?" As Ned grew more and more confident, I increased the choices to three, added matching, and occasionally asked a negative question: "Which one was *not* painted by Picasso?" These question sessions were the high point of my day. Now I could see why teachers like to test. It's very rewarding to see the results of your labors, to get proof that your lessons are really being absorbed. Of course, there was an Institutes rule that went with testing. Ned was *never* wrong. If he didn't choose the correct card, I would quickly put the right one in his hand, saying with a smile, "*This* one was painted in the fifteenth century." I asked him between fifteen and thirty questions daily, and he was able to give the correct answer without help a consistent 80 percent of the time. Not bad! And the questions kept getting harder.

This testing method was called "initial problem solving." Now we were beginning problem solving in a new way. In preparing Ned for our Italian travels, we had anticipated this next stage, which was called "intermediate problem solving." Relying on the same methods and materials we had been using all along in our intelligence sessions—bits of information, related sentences and words, homemade books—we would prepare Ned for two major projects weekly. One project had an academic goal and one a practical goal. Then on a weekend "culmination day" we would use the cards to prompt Ned through complex practical tasks or have him demonstrate academic knowledge in a more sophisticated way.

We started with a week in which the academic and practical projects were related. Ned learned to identify spring-flowering bulbs, matching them with pictures of the flowers they would produce, and with relevant fact cards. For his practical project he helped plant samples of each bulb in pots. His tongue stuck out slightly as he worked intently and seriously. It was the first time we had ever seen Ned settle down to an extended project in which he had to follow directions and work very carefully. He reminded us of the young Ned who had worked on his block constructions with such concentration, but now he was following our plans rather than his own. This culmination day led to a follow-up schedule of responsibilities. He checked on his bulbs to observe them for foliage growth, gave them additional water, and moved them into the light when they had sprouted sufficiently. We all watched with interest for the eventual flowers.

Each week we were thrilled with the abilities Ned was demonstrating in intermediate problem solving. He went on to learn about dinosaurs, how to play card games, bird identification, identifying the trees in the Arroyo, current events, how to pack a picnic lunch; with an appropriate culmination day sometimes at the zoo, planetarium, or a museum, sometimes with a demonstration of a new skill.

Dear Grammy: I played on the swing at the beach. Harry took me to the beach. We sat on the sand. We ate sandwiches. I made them myself. I saw a pelican and many seagulls, sandpipers, and dowitchers.

Love, Ned

Dear Grammy: I made a cheese sandwich. I put milk in the thermos bottle. I packed an apple for dessert. Mommy and I went to the Arroyo and had a picnic. We saw a hawk. We gave bread to the ducks.

Love, Ned

In the most complex and success culmination day of all, Ned planted a bulb garden near the front door. He removed the old plants, prepared the ground with a spade, added soil amendments, dug out six inches of this mixture, placed twenty dozen bulbs in the earth, covered them with the prepared soil, and raked it smooth. Finally, he planted a ground cover of fairy primroses. At each step I showed him the cards that had been his lessons during the week. He glanced at them and with verbal prompting and demonstrations by Bill on how to use the tools, he set to work. He toiled for five hours straight and was ready for the final step of watering. Ned held the hose as I turned on the water. I approached him to show him the last card, which read, "Next, we water the plants very gently." He averted his eyes from the card and then turned the hose on me, apparently having had enough for that day—enough of working and, especially, enough of me!

We sent the Institutes regular, detailed reports on our progress.

> *Pasadena, California*
> *November 4, 1980*

Miss Susan Aisen
The Institutes for the Achievement of Human Potential
8801 Stenton Avenue
Philadelphia, Pennsylvania

Dear Susie:
This week Ned learned about the election process, our government, and the political parties. By the end of the week he was able to identify the candidates for president, vice-president, senator, and congressman. He could identify the party symbols and associate campaign buttons, literature, bumper stickers, etc., with the appropriate candidate. As this was such sophisticated material, I did not ask Ned to verbalize his answers but to answer by choosing pictures, words, and phrases. His responses were 100 percent accurate. My questions to him used some materials he had not actually seen before, such as political cartoons. At the end of our session he "voted" for his choices. As part of this project Ned watched the presidential debate and has

seen part of the evening news each night. Today he will walk to the polls with us and see some of the returns on television.

Practical: We began to teach Ned about maps by making a map of our own neighborhood. Ned learned about street signs, directions, scale. However, the map concept is a difficult one, and we need additional practice. As Ned needs a run each day, we will continue to use the maps during his running time and plan to have another map project once we have established the basic concepts.

In addition to the above projects and his daily dictated letter and his weekly script, Ned is receiving math equations and story problems, spelling words, Italian lessons (he loves the Institutes tape!), and is hearing classical music during his bath. His household responsibilities are increasing continually. He now makes his bed and straightens his room, takes out the trash, sets the table, helps load the dishwasher, helps with food preparation, waters the potted plants, and sorts the laundry.

Very truly yours,
Barbara Christopher

Ned's "voting" in the election turned out to be surprisingly in the mainstream. He chose Republican Ronald Reagan for our new president and voted to reelect Democrat Alan Cranston as senator from California. And so did the majority of voters.

With all of this new activity, Ned still continued a strenuous physical program of crawling and creeping, but the activities of brachiation and running had achieved the status of rewards.

Dear Grammy:
I played on the ladder. I worked with my teacher, Stephanie. I ate grapefruit. I ran with Harry. I played with Pepper. I played Old Maid with Harry and Mommy.

Love, Ned

Things had never been better. We decided to do something we had wanted to do for years. We made reservations at the

Ahwahnee Hotel in Yosemite for Thanksgiving dinner. We reserved a cabin for a few days, and we all trooped to Yosemite for the holiday. En route we stopped at Bob's Big Boy for a snack, and I overheard two women talking. "Guess who's over there? Father Mulcahy and his three children." (Alan Alda had said that the program was making Bill smarter. Could it be that it was making me younger?) Yosemite was its immutable self, and we hiked through the woods and climbed to the top of Vernal Falls. On Thanksgiving Day we dressed up and walked to the Ahwahnee. We warmed ourselves in front of the huge fireplace in the lobby and then went into the spectacular dining room, one of the most beautiful rooms in the world. There were tall candles on every table reflecting the sparkling candle chandeliers. There was Chopin on the piano. Through the long windows we looked out on deer grazing in the dusk. Ned was perfectly behaved; we were perfectly happy.

Dear Grandpa Jim:
  Men are working upstairs. They are painting the living room.
It is white. The floor is wood. You will see it at Christmas.

Love, Ned

The holidays brought my mother and Jim, and they had a chance to see that Ned never behaved in Pasadena as he had at Kennedy Airport. They made special times for Ned, inviting him to our guest house, or the "Little House" as we call it, for lunch. Ned even paid attention to his grandmother's needs. She had been having trouble with her eyes, and he would walk ahead of her to turn on lights. (Four poker chips for that!)

Nineteen eighty had been our best year ever. In the very earliest hours of 1981, Bill and I walked along the boulevard watching the workers frantically putting finishing touches on the floats for the morning's parade. Another beautiful year was beginning in Pasadena. We felt serenely optimistic. Maybe, just maybe, Ned was going to make it, really make it. He had come so far in the past few years; he was learning to be aware of other people; he was happy and leading a productive life; he was able to show his intelligence in more and more ways. A dream was beginning to shape itself, a dream of a time when Ned might be able to live on his own, have a job, be normal or awfully close to it. Perhaps someday he could live in the "Little House" and take care of himself.

Many of our neighbors were out strolling the parade route too.

"Happy New Year, Christophers."

"Hi, Bill! Hi, Barbara. How are you?"

How were we? How was everything? *Molto bene, grazie.*

CHAPTER 8

Good-bye, Home

The first few days of 1981 were peaceful enough. Soon after New Year's Day, Betty and Jim returned to Glastonbury and I went back to work on "M*A*S*H." One morning when I had a late call at the studio, I sat in the kitchen with my coffee while Barbara stood poaching eggs for Ned's breakfast. He had been in his room dressing, and we heard his footsteps thumping down the uncarpeted stairs. He barreled into the kitchen, raced up to Barbara, and began to pinch her violently. He was highly agitated and crying loudly. When Barbara turned away he pursued her, pulling at her clothing and pinching wherever he could.

We were astonished. There had been the outburst of violence on our way back from Italy, but there was some excuse for that—fatigue and excitement, four weeks off the program. But here was Ned, after a good night's rest, months into his best program ever, on the attack. We reacted just as you might expect, with firm orders to stop that kind of behavior, to stop it right away, to understand that there would be no breakfast until he calmed down, to know that Mommy had gone upstairs and would not fix his breakfast unless he could behave himself. He did calm down as soon as Barbara left the room; within a short time she returned, and Ned had his breakfast as usual. I went off to work feeling uneasy, and by the time I arrived home that evening, Barbara was terribly upset. Ned had been attacking her, on and off, all day.

From that time on, even while doing the physical work of the program, there would be outbursts of this terrible behavior.

"You must understand, Ned, you cannot be allowed to hurt Mommy," I reasoned. "No, Ned!" Barbara shouted as he attempted to pinch her breasts. "Ned, go to your room. You may not even do your program unless you can behave like a civilized person," we threatened. "There will be no lunch today," we punished. Absolutely nothing worked—the cold shoulder, pleas, threats, withdrawing privileges—nothing at all.

Convinced that this was going to be a short-term problem, we developed a method of living with the behavior. Barbara, the only target at this point, would leave the room and someone else, usually Harry or Stephanie, would work with Ned. There were still some moments when Barbara could be with him, and then she tried to show him a lot of affection. Their best times together came when they were working on his intelligence program. Ned was still able to complete some complex projects—silk-screening valentines, learning to mop the floor, identifying the countries on the map of Europe—and to have successful question-answering sessions; but as the days wore on we began to realize that the hurtful behavior was not going to go away unless we got some help.

We called the Institutes. They suggested using the Civil Code and enforcing our family principles. We thought we had been doing that, but we determined to try harder. We wrote a new principle for Ned: "Ned is always kind and gentle." We presented a special lesson on behavior three times daily along with all his other lessons. We rewarded him heavily for good behavior and severely taxed him for pinching. But Ned didn't care at all. A carload of poker chips and all the privileges they would "buy" would not dissuade him from pinching and grabbing.

A number of times on my return from the studio, I heard Ned calling from his bedroom window, sometimes plaintively, sometimes cheerfully, "Hi, Daddy. Can I come out?" and I knew that Barbara had had to lock him in his room so that she could prepare dinner in safety. In order to protect herself from Ned's attacks while allowing him some freedom, Barbara would lock herself in our bedroom. When she had to be in his presence, she now wore a heavy coat buttoned to the chin.

Stephanie, who was standing shoulder to shoulder with us throughout this trying period, was very concerned about Barbara's safety. She took Barbara to a seminar offered by the school district on the management of assaultive behavior to learn physical holds and techniques for avoiding injury. A whole new world had opened up before us, a frightening and terrible world. There are many autistic kids who become violent during adolescence, but we had never thought it would happen in our family, to our Ned.

Ned was clearly unhappy when aggressing. More and more, he lived in a state of agitation and often had long sessions of loud, tearless crying. He didn't understand what was happening any more than we did. He was beginning to lash out at Stephanie and even Harry. Barbara was covered with bruises, and each day became more of a hurdle. "I've called the Jay Nolan Center for help," said Barbara.

The Jay Nolan Center provides a variety of services for the autistic and their families in the Los Angeles area and at this time had a federal grant for a pilot program to help families deal with unmanageable behaviors. By teaching good management techniques, the Jay Nolan Intensive Intervention Team had made it possible for nine families to keep their autistic children at home, an expectation we had always had for Ned. We would be their tenth and final family under this grant. After evaluating Ned and our situation, the team concluded that it should not be too difficult to get his behavior under control. They were impressed by the fact that Ned had such a structured life. Every moment of his day was accounted for; he was never at loose ends and was always involved with other people. They assured us this would be a great advantage in eliminating the problem. It was a matter of teaching us techniques and of showing Ned who was boss.

The interventionists began with a period of observation. For five days, from the moment Ned awakened until he was asleep for the night, at least one interventionist stayed with us, keeping data on Ned's aggression and on our reactions. At the outset they told us that we were demonstrating fear in our reactions to him. They showed us how to control our body

English so as to give the impression of unflappability. We were quick learners in that area. After all, actors are conscious of body language in their work, and Barbara and Harry too had studied for the stage.

The team members were intrigued with Ned's Institutes program and readily plunged in to help with patterning, but their clipboards were ever-present. At the end of a week they were ready to start us on a new way of reacting to Ned's assaults. When Ned attempted to aggress, he was asked to fold his hands. If he did this compliantly, he was allowed to resume working or eating or playing. If he did not fold his hands but continued to reach out in a hurtful way, he was asked to sit on the floor and be quiet for two minutes. Again, if compliant he was allowed to resume activities, but if not, he was asked to lie on the floor face down. In a calm voice he was told to relax; again, the object was to see him comply for two minutes. This was the ultimate stage, and when it was first employed, a gentle restraint was needed to keep Ned prone. When he became quiet, he was slowly released until he was ready to resume work. To begin with, the results appeared promising. Ned didn't seem to mind the interference. The pinching did continue, but at least we had a way of dealing with it.

The intervention team spent all day, every day, with us while we continued with a full Institutes program. They helped and were there to intervene when the assaultive behavior surfaced. We went to stores, restaurants, parks, playgrounds, museums, just as we had before the aggression began. And everywhere we went, a member of the intervention team went with us.

March 10, 1981

Dear Grammy,

I earned lunch at McDonald's by keeping control of myself. I ate hamburger at McDonald's. And I ate yellow French fries at McDonald's. I drank milk. Daddy and Leslie went to McDonald's.

Ned

GOOD-BYE, HOME

March 18, 1981

Dear Grammy,

Yesterday we went to Descanso Gardens. We saw fish swimming in the water. They were brown and gray. We went to the teahouse. We ate cookies. I drank red juice through a white straw. Mommy drank tea. Dave and Brad went with me.

Love, Ned

PS Love to Grandpa too.

The intervention team's evaluation of Ned included the phrase "mildly retarded." We always hated to hear Ned called retarded, not just because we didn't think it was true but because the next step was that he would lower himself to the expectations of those around him. We decided not to argue the point with them, but to let Ned change their minds with a demonstration of his intelligence.

"Which one of these sculptures is by Praxiteles?" Barbara asked Ned, showing him two cards. "Very good, Ned. You are absolutely correct." Ned responded to question after question with ready, non-verbal answers, picking up the correct cards. "Which one of these creatures lives in the sea?—Right again, Ned. You are great." And in case Al and Dave, standing by with their clipboards, weren't impressed enough with these answers, Barbara went on to see what would happen if she asked Ned to verbalize.

"Tell me about Rome."

There was a long pause. "Go to Rome with Mommy and Daddy."

"Yes, Ned! We all went together. Tell me what you liked best in Rome."

"You liked the restaurant." (Ned still had trouble with his pronouns.)

"You did, didn't you. I did too! What building did you like the best?"

"St. Peter's in the Vatican."

"Yes, that's a beautiful building. I liked it too. Do you remember who designed the dome?"

"Michelangelo."

"Did he really say that?" said Al. He did indeed. Ned was pretty smart. Unfortunately, too smart for the intervention program designed to control his behavior. After about two weeks Ned almost invariably pressed his aggression to the point where he was put on the floor with restraint. It was becoming a contest, as he began to resist. Soon more restraint was needed, and the duration grew longer and longer. Finally, there were times when Ned was held prone by two or three adults for hours on end. The team confidently assured us this would eventually lead to a controlled Ned. We hoped that it was so, but we began to wonder. Ned had begun to spit at those restraining him. If he could, he scratched and pinched the hands that held him. And soon he was biting. We had lost his trust. Where was the Ned of only a few months ago? "I think he's getting mad," said John, "and I'd be pretty mad too, if I were Ned."

We had always felt that John had handled the strain of having Ned as a brother extremely well. There had been a lot to put up with, of course, but all in all he had been able to have a pretty normal family life. But now we had a group of strangers continually in our midst. They were wonderful, hard-working, dedicated people who were trying to help us keep our family together, but their constant presence did alter the balance at home. Ned's aggression kept increasing. Barbara was frequently in tears. I was tense with worry. Home was absolutely awful. Everything had disintegrated into a terrible mess. Through it all we were doing our best to see that John had some chance to have fun with us, but those moments were too few. We felt grateful that at least he had his sports to turn to.

Pasadena, California
April 7, 1981

Dear Grandma,

How are you? The weather has been really great lately. I just finished basketball. We did well with a 9–4 record. Now I am playing baseball and starting at catcher on the varsity team. Unfortunately, our team is 0–3 but we have played the three best teams in the league. After our high school season is over I'm going to play Senior League for Pasadena. That team looks like it is going to be very good because I was on the same team last year and we have a lot of the same guys coming back.

I have been very busy lately, working very hard at school. I did have a few problems at the beginning of the year but seem to have everything under control now.

By the way, between now and the first paragraph our baseball team won a game 19–18 in which we were losing 18–3 with two innings to go. We scored seven runs in the sixth and eight runs in the seventh to force extra innings (six of the eight with two outs). Neither team scored in the eighth and we scored one in the bottom of the ninth to win.

Dad and I just returned from the Los Angeles Lakers basketball game which they lost on the last shot of the game.

Well, I have to go but I hope to see you soon.

Love, John

The intervention team was with us for four weeks, but in spite of their efforts, when their involvement with our family was over, Ned was worse off than he had been at the beginning. John had been right; Ned was not only aggressive, he was angry. He rarely attacked me, but Harry returned from running in the Arroyo with Ned, scratched and bitten. Sometimes Ned went after John. He became earnest in his efforts to hurt Stephanie. We finally devised a system so that Stephanie could keep working with Ned. We locked him in a first-floor room and she sat outside the window, giving him spelling words, math problems, and reading lessons through the screen. The barrier had a calming effect, and Ned was able to do his work. At least, I thought, he doesn't really want to hurt people. For some reason he just can't help himself.

We continued to use the intervention team's methods, more out of desperation than confidence, but we needed two people if we were to do the prone restraint, and with the intervention team's departure, we were sometimes shorthanded. There were many times when John had to help restrain his brother. What must this be doing to him? To all of us?

There was a closing party for the end of the ninth "M*A*S*H" season, and the next day we took John to San Diego and Baja California for a week's vacation. We were trying to restore some kind of sanity to our family. We offered him Hawaii, but he said, "Let's go to Hawaii some other year." Yes, we would go some other year, when things were better. Harry the stalwart took charge of Ned and home; Jennifer and Brad from the intervention team returned to help him; and a couple trained to provide respite to families like ours spelled them. The three of us had a good rest and enjoyed each other's company. But when we returned, things were just the same, or somewhat worse. A week away from Ned enabled us to see him more clearly. He had always been particularly healthy, but over the past few months he had lost weight. He looked emaciated. His complexion, which had always been glowingly pink, was tinged with blue. He had always been very active, but now he was spending time with a blanket pulled over his head, depressed and withdrawn.

During our absence Ned had received a terrible burn on his leg. It had occurred on the respite couple's shift, and we never did get a clear story about what had happened. It was a severe burn, blistered and oozing, but Ned was oblivious to it. He expressed no pain at all, even when the doctor pulled off the bandage. There must be something else going on with Ned, I thought. Something more than just unacceptable behavior.

We called the Institutes again, and they suggested we come to Philadelphia and plan to stay several weeks. Occasionally families who had arrived at a roadblock in their programs stayed at the Institutes at no additional cost while the staff tried to solve the problem. Prior to the visit they wanted neurological tests to rule out gross physiological causes.

Pasadena, California
May 8, 1981

Dear Grandma and Grandpa Jim,
Thank you very much for the money that you sent for Easter and my birthday. I am sure that I will be able to put it to good use.

I have been keeping busy with school and sports. My Dad took Ned for testing at the hospital but they didn't find anything, so I don't know what is going to happen.

I will see you this summer.

Love, John

As expected, Ned's brain looked perfectly normal in EEG and CAT scans, although it had taken massive amounts of tranquilizers and total anesthesia to make the tests possible. But at last we were ready to go back to Philadelphia. We had the greatest faith in the Institutes and believed that they could help us if anyone could.

Pasadena, California
May 9, 1981

Dear Mother:

Thank you for the very, very generous birthday gifts. I bought Ned some cute shirts for the trip to Philadelphia but am waiting to shop for myself when I return. Bill will stay on in Philadelphia with Ned as long as the Institutes staff think necessary, and I will have a couple of weeks home alone with John, with days totally free. (I can hardly believe it!)

Some good news: Ned's brain scan was normal. Also, the neurologist was finally able to come up with an effective tranquilizer, so the trip doesn't seem quite so daunting.

Harry and John are confident that they can manage alone while I'm away.

Much love and in haste, Barbara

PS Happy Mother's Day

On Ned's thirteenth birthday we left for Philadelphia. A neurologist in Pasadena had prescribed Haldol for the flight. It had worked perfectly well in a trial dosage. She prescribed six tablets to be administered throughout the trip. Barbara gave him the first one just before boarding and almost immediately after takeoff he had a frightening reaction. He went into a kind of trance. His mouth hung open, his back was arched, and for hours his hand with the index finger extended stayed up in the air over his head. His breathing was shallow; his leg was drawn up; he stared like a zombie. When the flight finally ended, I half-carried Ned off the plane. In panic we called Dr. Wilkinson at the Institutes. She reassured us: "Give him lots of water to drink and let him sleep it off." He gradually recovered, but it took three days for him to get over it completely.

Our first week at the Institutes was similar in structure to our former visits. We joined another kumi and went through all of the meetings, lectures, and evaluations. After a few days we moved onto the Institutes grounds. This would give the staff a chance to see Ned in a wider variety of situations. In an effort to see whether it might affect his aggression, Ned's diet was changed to one of complete foods: raw peas, raw beans, almonds, hazelnuts. There were metabolic studies, consultations with a neurologist and an endocrinologist, and a glucose-tolerance test. But as usual, these tests showed nothing abnormal, nothing that gave any clue to what had gone wrong.

After we had been there a week, Barbara returned to Pasadena to be with John, and Ned and I continued to share a third-floor bedroom in the main building of the Institutes. We rose early each morning and suited up. We both had Institutes outfits: tee shirt, shorts, high-topped gym shoes, a dark blue one-piece coverall, and kneepads. The staff felt it was urgent that Ned get back to as intense a program as possible. And to make it work, I did a great deal of it with him. After a simple breakfast, we started every day on the "human development course." This was the area where the resident students did their physical program, a paved section behind the main building marked out for creeping, crawling, rolling, jumping, brachiation, somersaulting. When the students had finished their chores, they joined us, and we all worked together for the rest of the morning. In the afternoon Ned and I attended their intelligence program classes and then participated in the daily run, sometimes cross-country, sometimes at a track. Ned masked every seven minutes. I kept my clipboard records at all times and carried a bag of fruit and vegetable snacks to get him

(Above) Barbara showing Ned word cards in the middle of a creeping session. Pepper poses. 1978.

(Below) Bill getting ready to join Ned creeping. 1978.

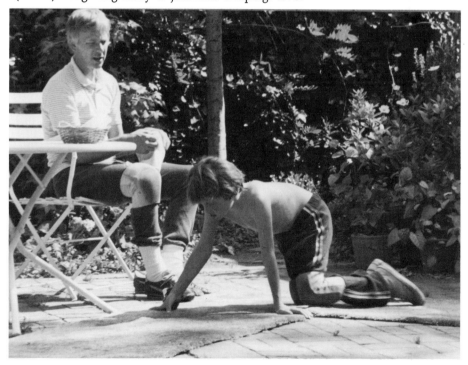

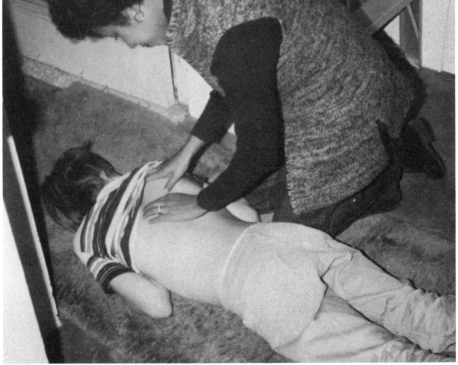

(Above left) The fatal dish of ice cream. Rome, 1980.

(Below left) Stephanie giving a five-minute tactile session as part of Ned's last Institutes program. Fall 1980.

(Below) Ned riding in a gondola on the Grand Canal in Venice. Spring 1980.

(Above) Ned on a home visit from Vista House. 1981.

(Left) Grammy visiting Ned at Devereux in October 1983. Ned is wearing the "Goodbye, Farewell, and Amen" tee shirt from the final episode of "M*A*S*H."

(Above right) Ned as an angel strides across the Devereux campus. Halloween 1984.

(Below right) John on the day of his high school graduation. June 1984.

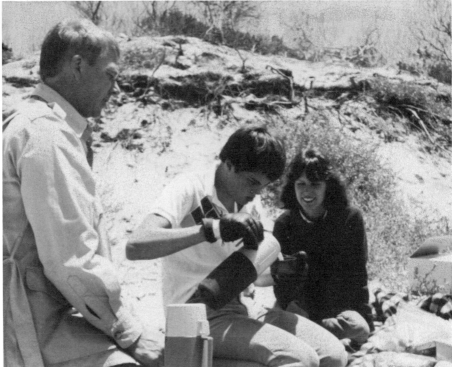

(Above left) Ned doing some cooking on a home visit from Devereux. 1985.

(Below left) A picnic on the beach near Devereux with Bill and Alice. Ned is wearing his "magic gloves." 1985.

(Above) Ned home for his eighteenth birthday. 1986.

(Above) Ned jumping into "cold Lee's pool." 1987.

(Left) Ned on his nineteenth birthday, looking at a new book with Bill. 1987.

(Above right) Ned at his 4H riding program, rubbing Frosty's back. 1987.

(Below right) Ned still enjoys tactile input. Home, February 1988.

(Above) Ned and Barbara outside Ned's Devereux classroom. April 1988.

(Right) Ned running on the beach. 1986.

(Above) Just out of the hot tub on a home visit. Ned still likes to tear leaves and twigs. May 1988.

(Left) Ned hiking in the Arroyo. May 1988.

(Above) On the Devereux campus. August 1985.

through each day. It was a rain or shine program. Sometimes we broiled in the sun; sometimes we were drenched to the skin. Ned worked through it all. The staff got to know him well, his aggressions, his moods, his flashes of keen intelligence, and his ability to work hard. Every night we staggered exhausted up to our room, where Ned fell asleep and I read Henry James, resting my tired body and brain with the soothing picture of Roderick Hudson's Rome. It helped to think of Rome, its beauty and the Ned who had been with us there.

Ned sometimes got into trouble at the evening meal, which he and I took with the students. He grabbed at the girls, pulled hair, or took food from other plates. He shouted belligerently when he was corrected: "You don't have to sit down. No sit down." Or sometimes even when someone greeted him: "No Hi. No Hi, Ned." Whenever Ned's behavior disrupted the meals or the classroom, we had to remove ourselves. But time after time, day after day, we were welcomed back to try again. The staff did what they could to make Ned a part of the student life, encouraging his participation at all times. They provided me with constant ideas and support. To meet his need for intense tactile stimulation, I did salt rubs on Ned's legs each night before bed. The staff showed me a positive way of treating Ned's aggression by roughhousing with him. Slowly Ned did begin to improve.

Ned and I stayed at the Institutes a total of six weeks. At the end of that time I felt encouraged that the aggression could be overcome. Ned's improvement during the intense weeks of work with the students had indicated that to me and to the staff. We left with a very encouraging program. Ned was to duplicate at home as nearly as possible the work done by the resident students at the Institutes. Then, if he could accomplish the degree of independence needed to live with the students, he would begin the transition to being a resident student himself. We were terribly excited by this prospect. The plan was for us to return to the Institutes in October for another stay, this time for two weeks. Then at three-month intervals, Ned would stay for longer and longer periods, until eventually he would be ready to live at the Institutes full time.

The primary goal of Ned's new program was to regain optimum health. To help him gain weight and to lessen aggression—hungry people are more aggressive—he was to have meals or very heavy snacks every two hours. His vitamin program was upped to an anti-stress level. Another goal was appropriate tactile sensation. The Institutes thought that Ned's lack of tactile awareness was a contributing factor in his aggression. His reaction to pain and light touch had always been abnormal and during this period had become even more so. The main technique addressing this deficit was tactile stimulation performed in a variety of ways: We were to brush, tap, and stroke Ned with a Dobie, a kind of pot scrubber for Teflon-coated cookware—in other words rough but not too rough. So that he could have an all-over tactile experience, there was to be regular roughhousing. He was to be massaged gently but with firm pressure. There would be hugging, stroking, rubbing, varying in intensity from rough to gentle. All of this was to be done twelve times a day in five-minute sessions.

Using our Institutes day as a model, we set up our new schedule. At seven o'clock Ned would get up and dress in running clothes. He then had breakfast and vitamins, helped clean up after breakfast, and straightened his room. By eight-thirty he was ready for his intelligence hour. Barbara had lessons set up in three locations: the dining room, the kitchen, and Ned's room. Each fifteen minutes Ned moved to a different location. There was a small ceremony of greeting and masking:

"Welcome to your lesson on American history. It's time to mask."

Ned put on his mask and Barbara timed him.

"Unmask."

Ned removed his mask.

"It's time to sit at the table."

Ned then had a series of lessons organized around a particular subject.

"Your lesson on American history is over. You may stand."

"Thank you, Mommy."

In each section we would use bits of information, reading cards, writing lessons, and math. The lessons in each fifteen-minute section would grow harder. We would end the hour asking Ned questions based on the materials. After completing his intelligence hour, Ned had a light snack and juice, and then we set off on a five-mile run. When we returned from running, Ned showered and dressed in his blue Institutes coverall and then had his lunch and vitamins. From noon to four-thirty Ned worked on our "human development course" (we had marked out a course in our yard similar to the one at the Institutes). Dressed for work and with kneepads in place, Ned would alternate between crawling, creeping, and brachiation. He would have snacks and juice as he worked. At four-thirty Ned would be through with the hardest part of the day. He would dress for swimming and put his work clothes in the washing machine. He could then swim for half an hour in Lee's pool. Ned set the table for dinner and helped with food preparation. Following dinner and vitamins, he could choose a reward. By eight-thirty he had bathed and was in bed. Throughout the day the schedule was interrupted for tactile input and masking.

On weekends Ned was to work on the "human development course" for two hours and then go to the beach and accomplish ten miles of running in what was left of the day. Between stretches of running, he could swim and play in the sand.

Determined to have hope, we plunged into this program. If we could only get Ned prepared to live at the Institutes, then we could be assured of his continued progress without having to be responsible for every minute ourselves. But things weren't easy. Ned continued to be aggressive, and home was far from relaxed. We packed John off to Glastonbury. There at least, he could have the undivided attention of people who loved him.

For ourselves, we tried grabbing one of those holds upon happiness. I had the distraction and reward of days on the set, another world to escape to, the companionship of those who knew nothing of our troubles. But Barbara, against whom the major part of Ned's aggression was directed, was badly in need of something very special. I wanted us to have some time together and alone. Some months earlier I had arranged a vacation for us in Europe. Unexpectedly and wonderfully, we were still able to work it out, and we left Ned and the program in Harry's capable hands for two whole weeks.

London
June 29, 1981

Dear Mother and Jim:
We arrived yesterday. The plane was very cramped but I slept anyway. We went into London for dinner and walking around and today we are going to St. Paul's Cathedral and some more walking before we leave for Venice. The days are very long: sunrise 4:30 A.M., sunset 9:30 P.M. Had a great dinner—Indian (Punjab) food—most unusual. Great idea, traveling without children!

Love, B.

Venice
July 1, 1981

Dear Mother and Jim:
Here we are in Venice. Absolutely wonderful. Not nearly as crowded as last year. Blooming window boxes everywhere and lovely weather. Today we walked and rode on the water ferry around to many of the beautiful churches. In between churches, we ate and ate and ate. We just had coffee and ice cream at Florian's and it's 1:00 A.M. Tomorrow we board the Sea Cloud.

B.

Sicily
July 7, 1981

Dear Mother and Jim:
Etna wasn't doing much when we saw it from the boat. We were enjoying ourselves very much in Palermo when I was mugged! I hung on to my purse but was shaken up. We had a wonderful day

*in charming Amalfi and are now headed for our last stop, London
and home. It has been great.*

Love, B.

It *was* great. A great respite, but only that. We were soon
back home and facing the same problems. The program was
more demanding than ever, and we were constantly fighting
off Ned's aggression. Without the atmosphere of the Institutes
and the inspiring example of the students and staff there, the
"human development course" seemed endless. And although
Ned accomplished it daily, there was the continual threat of
violence. We were always tense and on the alert.

At the end of August we escaped to Balboa again, and Ned
did fairly well there. Our neighbors along the Grand Canal, as
the island waterway is called, took a great interest in Ned. They
watched as John or Harry or I played with him in the water or
chased him along the beach. Mrs. Eubanks, our neighbor on
one side, offered Ned cookies and shrugged off a pinch on the
arm. "That's all right, dear," she said to Barbara, who ran up to
her to apologize. "I know you're having a hard time. But he's a
dear, sweet little boy." Jim White, on the other side, offered us
a rowboat, and Ned and I put on many miles circling the tiny
island. Jim didn't mind that Ned liked to climb on his
catamaran and jump off into the water. We could not have
encountered a more sympathetic group of people.

Fortunately, Ned's aggression was usually reserved for
family members. But we kept up a constant vigil. I watched
Ned approach some kids on the shore and ran toward them. I
was always afraid he might hurt or frighten someone. I
explained to the children that Ned was having a hard time
these days and sometimes pinched people. "That's okay,"
they said nonchalantly. "We've seen Ned here every summer.
He won't hurt us." And he didn't. But I never relaxed, not for a
moment.

We accomplished the two weeks at Balboa; Ned was brown
and healthy; John had enjoyed his friends and the surf. But it
had hardly been a vacation for Barbara and me. Back home

the tension of living with Ned, not knowing when he might explode, being afraid to have anyone alone with him, warning strangers away from him, planning every outing with the strategy of a general, finally giving up going out in public entirely, was too much for us.

We realized that we could not go on with this way of life. It was just too difficult. Ned was going to have to leave home. We would give up our wonderful dreams of a normal life for him. We would give up the idea of success the Institutes way. We would give up the plan for Ned taking his place among the hard-working Institutes students whom we admired so much. With heavy hearts we called Philadelphia. Ned was going off program. He would not be returning in October. He was going to live in a community-based group home and go to public school, and we would hope for the best.

Ned's seat belt was securely fastened. His things, all marked with his name, were packed in the trunk of the car. He was starting a new life. We had explained to him what was happening. He didn't cry, but he looked apprehensive as I pulled out of the driveway. "Wave to Mommy, Ned."

"Good-bye, Mommy."

"Good-bye, Ned."

"Good-bye, home."

CHAPTER 9

Searching

M argarita had helped me get ready for that day, preparing Ned's things for his move away from home. Laundry and labels, a few things to make his new room feel homey, new socks and underwear. It was not the cheerful preparation that had gone into John's departures for camp; it was a silent, diligent effort not to feel what we were both feeling. I drove her home when the day was done, and as I pulled the car up outside her house, she put her arms around me. We sat together for a long time, both crying. Margarita and I did not have much common spoken language, but we didn't need words very often and not at all that day. What was there to say, after all? In her years of working for our family, Margarita had watched Ned grow from a six-year-old into a rangy young adolescent. She had watched the hard work of his Institutes program; she had loved him and played with him and cooked special Mexican dishes for him. She was losing him too. And as a loving mother herself, she understood my loss. Ned was leaving home, not to return. What was I going to do with all the love I had for him?

In September, Bill and I had turned to the Lanterman Regional Center, desperately seeking help in finding a residential placement for Ned. California's system for providing information and services for the developmentally disabled is organized regionally, and Lanterman, our branch, was the obvious place for us to turn. They considered our situation an emergency, and Carolyn Carney, who had been assigned as our caseworker, was on the phone to me immediately. She heard a brief summary of our story and treated it with the utmost seriousness. She wanted to meet us face to face and to meet Ned. We set a date for her to come to our house, and before hanging up she said, "I'm blind. I hope that doesn't bother you." We are so used to people saying that they are blind ("I'm blind as a bat, you know") that I wasn't really sure I understood.

"Really blind?" I asked.

"Yes, completely."

But Carolyn is a farseeing woman. She was chauffeured to our house by her father. Ned looked at him and said, "Hi, Grandpa Jim." (And Carolyn's father does indeed look very much like Ned's grandpa, and sounds like him too, with his nice New England accent.) Carolyn sat on our living room sofa and heard all about Ned. She talked to Ned and, with a remnant of that sensitivity that he had developed before this awful change had struck him, Ned did not attempt to pinch her. She spoke bluntly about the extreme shortage of placements for adolescent autistic boys, particularly those who are aggressive. But with a thoroughly practical attitude she said, "But we are going to have to find some place for him. This situation at home cannot go on any longer." She was worried about us and worried about John.

Carolyn made phone call after phone call in Ned's behalf and gave me a list of places I could call to find out more about available programs. Although it was her job to find a placement, she knew that I would feel better if I had a chance to talk to admissions offices and social workers myself. I made a number of calls, one of them to the Devereux Foundation in Santa Barbara. Devereux is a well-known organization with campuses all over the country providing programs for the mentally ill and developmentally disabled. Margaret Curtice in the admissions department there was my first contact with the world of residential placement. She gave me many hours on the telephone, and her help and sympathy for our situation were a great comfort. She suggested other facilities to call but was afraid that Devereux in Santa Barbara did not have a program for Ned. She did send an application, but before I filled it out, Carolyn had found a group home about an hours drive from Pasadena. It was called Vista House, and they could take him right away.

Never before had we considered placing Ned out of our home. We had worked as hard as we knew how to offer him a normal life, to offer him a variety of experiences; and even after Ned became aggressive, I had been confident that we could continue to do so. All during our work with the intervention team, and during Bill's long stay at the Institutes, and for a while after the two of them returned from Philadelphia, I had had this confidence. Our failure weighed me down and sent me to my bed each night aching for sleep and able only to cry and lie awake staring at the ceiling. It couldn't have happened, not to Ned, not to my beautiful boy who could do so much, who surprised everyone with his abilities, who was now going to live with a group of strangers.

Ned was gone, and we weren't to see him for a month. One of the rules that often exists in placing children in residential facilities is a waiting period before visits are allowed. This is to establish the idea that the child does indeed now live somewhere else. As if there could possibly be any doubt about that in our minds. The dinner table was abnormally quiet. John now had a greater share of our attention than he really wanted. For over thirteen years we had been four, and now we were three, an awkward number. A terrible hole existed for us all.

The structure of the Institutes program was gone, and I was left to fill the empty hours. Bill had his work, and John had school and sports. I threw myself into an orgy of cleaning and straightening. I turned out the drawers and closets; I rearranged the furniture; I tidied everything. I wiped the fingerprints off the woodwork and removed the frieze of hand marks from the stairwell. How often I had wished for clean walls, but now they looked unnaturally clean to me, inhumanly clean. I shopped too, replacing the kitchen knives that Ned had damaged in his attempts at slicing or in his autistic exploration of the limits of their flexibility. I replaced all of my kitchen gadgets, rearranged the cupboards. A mysterious phenomenon appeared. The doors and drawers in the kitchen were continually agape. Apparently Ned had been the one in the family who kept them closed, the one who had assumed responsibility for a tidy kitchen. I had my hair cut and bought new clothes. I weeded and cultivated the garden. At night I lay in bed exhausted but unable to sleep. And I cried. There was no solace.

It was impossible to imagine what Ned must have been thinking and feeling at this sudden change in his life, and I tried not to think about it. When the waiting period was finally over and Ned began to come home for semi-weekly over-nights, he was shocked to find that I had purchased new flatware. He checked the silverware drawer, found that I had not arranged it to his liking, and rearranged it in a more pleasing manner. That was okay with me. After all, this was still his home, his ideas were still valuable. I was amused at his proprietary interest. I had moved the brass candlesticks from one side of the dining room to another. That wouldn't do, thought Ned. He carefully moved them to the precise spot where they had been before he left home. We smiled. Upstairs he found that the antique clock in the den had been moved from the top of one bookcase to the top of another. More work for Ned. He gently moved it, carrying the heavy old case with its iron weights and wooden works and putting it in its "proper" place. This was autistic behavior right out of the book, but Ned, unlike the other autistic kids we had read about, didn't mind when his rearrangements were disturbed. "Ned, Mommy and Daddy want the clock over there." Oh, okay. Back it went. He cheerfully accepted our explanation. But explanations were necessary. We would have to remember that. Let's keep Ned informed, let's not forget to tell him what to expect.

Our life settled into new patterns, and on the whole we felt that we had done the right thing, the only thing. And at first Ned seemed to do well enough and to be happy enough in his new life.

Pasadena, California
January 10, 1982

Dear Joan:
I have tried to call you several times without an answer and so am forced to take the extreme measure of putting pen to paper. We

had absolutely wonderful holidays, very relaxed and festive, a difficult balance to achieve. I was very glad to see the end of 1981, which was the worst year of my life, and so far 1982 (all ten days' worth) has been great. Ned has settled into his new home and new school pretty well and enjoys his visits here very much. The change in our family life has been enormous, and although the first few months were very rough for us, I do feel it has been a change for everyone's benefit.

Are you and Roger coming out in February? I seem to remember a plan to that effect. I do hope so. We would love to see you.

Meanwhile, much love and happiness in the New Year to you all.

B.

There was an initial period of enormous relief at not having to deal with the intensity of Ned's aggressive behaviors. But as we settled into the New Year, we took a hard look at Vista House and began to realize that the life there was woefully inadequate. On those alternate Sundays when Bill returned from driving Ned back to Vista House, he would be white-faced and grim. The people who staffed Vista House were well-meaning enough, almost everyone who works with handicapped children is, but they had absolutely no idea what to do with Ned. The house was in an ordinary neighborhood, but there was little or no contact with the neighbors. A small concrete back yard was the only outdoor area. There were a few balls and toy cars, but for the most part the kids and staff sat around while the TV blared. The principal program seemed to be for Ned to sit in a chair and be good. The poverty of the life appalled us. Ned had gone from a highly enriched, highly structured home life into a setting that was custodial at best. Something would have to change. But having made the break, a break that we knew was necessary for the health of everyone else in the family, we could not risk confusing Ned and ourselves by bringing him home only to have to send him away again, go through it all over again.

I pinned my hopes on the public school program to bring

some ray of light into Ned's life. I attended Ned's first IEP (Individualized Education Program), a meeting to outline educational priorities, and sat with the teacher, school administrator, psychologist, and speech therapist discussing Ned's educational background. The school insisted that although we could have educational goals for Ned, we could not really expect teachers to do much with our son until his behavior was "under control."

"I believe that unless Ned has plenty of content in his program, his aggression will only get worse," I said. "I have taught him at home for several years. And since his aggression began, the best times we have had together are when he is doing good, high-level work." I was not really listened to, and I knew it. But I was still too stunned at that point to be as persistent as I should have been. Spoiled by my long exposure to the Institutes, where parents were listened to and believed, I did not recognize that now I was going to have to fight for my views and for Ned. And I simply didn't realize that no one believed me when I told them what Ned had been capable of at home.

The classroom was not dingy; it did not lack clean, new furnishings; but to me it was a horror. Ned sat behind screens, partitioned off from the other children. Several of the kids in the class wore helmets to prevent self-injurious behavior. There was a low level of expectation for all of them, and for Ned, a plummet of expectation from the high of the Institutes intelligence program to a low of stringing beads. It was a non-verbal group, and Ned had no real academic program. The tasks he was assigned were things he had been able to do as a tiny child. And of course, he lowered himself to these lowered expectations. He threw the beads and pinched the teacher. He bit and scratched and spat. He misbehaved on the bus. Many days he did not make it to school at all, and as Vista House had no day program, when Ned did not go to school, he did nothing all day long.

Of course, we couldn't be satisfied with Vista House. It just wouldn't do. It operated within the rules imposed on group homes, but it simply wasn't up to our standards. Carolyn Carney was sympathetic, but told us we must recognize that there were very, very few places that would consider taking Ned, none that she knew of with an opening.

We tried desperately to make things better. First, I communicated some of the Institutes ideas to the staff at the group home. I delivered packages of my homemade intelligence materials and a couple of the staff did take an interest. I'm sure they found, as we had, that having something to do, something planned, was always a help in maintaining a reasonable relationship with Ned. But at best it was a gesture at something better. Then I visited his school and pleaded with the teacher to begin to give Ned some content in his school program. The teacher seemed sympathetic but very little changed for Ned.

I began to wonder if my efforts to communicate my ideas about education to Ned's teacher weren't self-defeating. Here was I trying to tell him that Ned could read and learn about art and history, quote poetry, speak a few words of Italian, and the teacher was interested in compliance tasks like sorting colored paper clips. I consulted with Stephanie, who knew Ned and his home program so well and who also taught a lively, interesting special education class in our local high school. She might have some ideas about traditional school programs that would prove more acceptable to Ned's teacher. I passed on her thoughts about reading, writing, and math approaches that might work for Ned, but somehow nothing much happened.

We began to receive communications that made us very uneasy.

Re: Ned Christopher
Since the elimination of medication at school he has become much more aggressive and generally out of control, more hallucinating and general non-compliance. He takes extreme amount of time to complete tasks, walk to bathroom and toilet. Much pinching, body contortion, not with the here and now, non-compliance, not staying in seat, spitting, loud noise, falling on knees.

Ned had been started on Mellaril the previous fall when we were still planning to take him back to Philadelphia. Dr.

Wilkinson of the Institutes had prescribed a moderate dose, and it had calmed Ned down and made it possible to consider taking him on the plane. It had never been part of the plan for him to stay on Mellaril for a prolonged period, but when we decided to send Ned to Vista House, they felt it was not a good time to reduce medication. Later when reductions were attempted, there were so many behavior problems that full dosage was resumed almost immediately.

Even in the worst of situations there are people who make a difference. Kate, the behavior management consultant at Vista House, was bright and creative. She came to visit when Ned was home for the weekend and taught us a valuable tool for dealing with his aggressions. It was the elimination of undesirable behavior by the technique of totally ignoring it. This technique was called "putting a behavior on extinction" or simply "extinction." Total ignoring is not as easy as it sounds and involves complete physical and mental control so as to communicate no response to inappropriate or aggressive behavior. This tool worked very well for us and was to serve us for years. Again, our acting training came into play. It was acting to turn away from Ned after he had pinched me and continue sorting the laundry, humming to myself. And acting again to turn back to him smiling and praising him for his good table manners or to chat with him about the weather, while in truth my heart was pounding and I was silently praying that he would not attack. But from the day that we learned about "extinction," I had very few pinches, and my times with Ned when he was home became better and better.

By March we had determined to find another place for Ned. We were over the shock of parting with him. We felt we had done the right thing, but we could not allow the present situation to continue. We applied to the Jay Nolan Center. Although all of their group homes had been full earlier when we needed a place for Ned, Carolyn had called to tell us that they were opening a new home and there might be room for him now. We waited breathlessly for a reply, and when it came, we found that ironically Ned had been rejected because he was already in a group home and there were others in greater need of placement. Of course, he would go on the waiting list.

I had been calling Mrs. Curtice at Devereux from time to time to tell her how things were going with Ned at Vista House, and as she sensed our growing dissatisfaction, she suggested that we come up and look at the Devereux campus and observe the programs to see if we thought Ned would be able to function well there. Carolyn thought this was a good idea. Just at that time, Liz was visiting us from Philadelphia, and we welcomed the opportunity of having a third opinion from someone who had been so intimately connected with our Institutes program and who knew Ned so well. The three of us drove along the California coast one breezy spring day to Santa Barbara. We drove out along an estuary, set aside as a bird sanctuary, onto the Devereux campus. Mrs. Curtice met us and took us around to the classrooms, vocational programs, the dorms, and the dining room, and we were impressed by it all. It is a large campus, and we didn't see all of the programs, but the classes we did visit were geared to kids with problems that seemed relatively minor compared with Ned's. It was heartening to see the caring atmosphere, the cheerful busy staff and kids, the beautiful surroundings, but it didn't really look possible for Ned. Or did it? On the return trip we talked about whether Ned could possibly fit in at Devereux. Liz, whose career in social work had given her a lot of experience with residential special schools, commented that the model of social behavior was excellent and that Ned could benefit greatly from that. I agreed but couldn't see how he could manage the level of compliance required in the classrooms. Bill thought that most of the kids were engaging in activities that Ned couldn't share: drama class, woodshop, bike riding. For 110 miles we discussed the possibilities and the difficulties. We carried an application form away with us, but it sat on my desk. I couldn't bear to fill it out only to have Ned rejected, couldn't bear to go through all the details of his life yet again. When did he sit up? When did he stand?

Perhaps we could work harder to help strengthen the program at Vista House. Ned was scheduled to change schools next year, and we had met his new teacher. She was very interested in him and agreed there had to be more content in his school day. She also expressed enthusiasm when we described his Institutes intelligence program, and that seemed a very good sign to us.

While we were struggling with trying to improve Ned's program, life, of course, was going on. Bill and I were off to New York for CBS. It was the tenth season of "M*A*S*H," and the cast was to be honored at a party. Everyone expected this to be the last season. The actors were presented with gold dog tags as mementoes of the occasion. We stayed at the Plaza, of course. "How's your boy doing?" asked the bell captain. It had been five years, and he remembered us and Ned!

When we returned home, something occurred that had me on the phone to Mrs. Curtice immediately. Ned was in the hospital. He had a fractured skull. Worse, he had had a fractured skull for five days before a doctor was called. I rushed to the hospital and was met by a steely-eyed doctor who clearly thought it was all my fault for having Ned living away from home. I was trying not to think so too. Ned had a black eye extending from his hairline to his chest. It was his second hospitalization since leaving home. The first time he had had a skin infection brought on by a gentle but insistent slapping of his face, a behavior that had spontaneously disappeared. He had never been a head-banger, and I did not believe that he had caused the skull fracture himself. Although I was told by the staff at Vista House that Ned had taken to banging his head on the wall, I had never seen it, and I simply didn't believe it.

In her charming Virginia accent, Mrs. Curtice said, "Miz Christopher, you had better bring that young man up here and let us meet him. Now I don't believe you ever sent me that completed application form." She was right, I hadn't. But I filled it out immediately and sent it off, and by the time Ned recovered from his skull fracture, Devereux was ready to meet him.

Meanwhile Vista House had decided that they had had enough of the Christopher family. We had been doing a great deal of complaining, and Ned wasn't getting any easier for them. In a dreadful meeting with the administrators, we were informed that as soon as another placement could be found, Ned would have to leave. That was all right with us. We didn't want him there another day, but returning home was also out of the question. We couldn't have him think that he was moving back with us and then send him away again. We can all only stand so much emotional pain.

Ned came home for a three-day weekend, and on Monday Bill and I drove him up to Devereux to face the inevitable interviews. We crossed our fingers that they would see fit to admit him. Ned was at his worst—on the attack, distributing pinches wherever he could, and running all over the place. We were greeted on our arrival by Tom, the residential supervisor of the dorm being considered for Ned, and by Michael, the psychologist assigned to that group of kids. They said they would look out for Ned while Bill and I began the preliminary paperwork with Mrs. Curtice, but in no time, they were in the office, laughing and saying, "Mr. Christopher, we apparently need your help." Bill, with what seemed a magic touch, walked Ned about the campus with them, chatting about how we usually handled the behaviors. Nervously, I filled out forms and talked to Mrs. Curtice. Finally, we all sat together and had a chance to go over Ned's fourteen-year history. To our amazement, Tom asked, "What would be best for you? To have him start on Wednesday or Friday?" Ned had been accepted at Devereux for a three-month trial period. They had seen him at his worst and still thought they could work with him. He would never have to go back to Vista House again!

Pasadena, California
June 28, 1982

Dear Mother:

Ned is safely ensconced at Devereux and the relief is, as you can imagine, wonderful. Of course, it is only a probationary period and we will just have to keep our fingers crossed that it will go well, or well enough for him to stay there. It will be three months before a final decision is made.

Things are getting off to a rather rough start, but no one appears terribly surprised at that. Ned enjoys the spacious campus and taking walks. And, as always, he enjoys eating! You can write to him at the Devereux Foundation, Box 1079, Santa Barbara 93102.

I have a lot of confidence in the people at Devereux. The staff are thoughtful, caring, intelligent, have good backgrounds and they like Ned. Ned looks great. He's smiling again and has gained weight.

We are going on a vacation to Greece, celebrating the above. (And also the good news that "M*A*S*H" is going into an eleventh season!) John will stay with his coach and go to a baseball clinic at Pepperdine University. Then he will fly to Denver to meet Louise and Chris and drive with them to Peoria for a family reunion at Bill's brother's house. We'll hook up with John and all the Christophers there on our way home from Greece.

All sounds pretty wonderful, doesn't it? It's a long time since you have had such a cheerful letter from me. Or any letter at all, for that matter.

L. & K., B.

The relief was unbelievable. Ned was enrolled at Devereux in a program that had a solid reputation behind it, run by a foundation that had been providing good programs for seventy years. I felt relaxed, as I had not in months. I began to study maps and guidebooks, and Bill rushed off to Berlitz in an attempt to modernize his Homeric Greek.

July 27, 1982
Mykonos

Dear Mother and Jim:
This card shows part of a Byzantine ghost town we visited three days ago. It seems hard to find the time to write cards. We are so busy looking at things. Today we are on Mykonos, a kind of Greek Balboa Island, with pretty views, charming houses, and cute shops. We have done a lot of driving through beautiful countryside and have seen a lot of ruins, and now it is very pleasant to sit still on a little balcony and look at the blue Aegean.

B.

Pasadena, California
August 14, 1982

Dear Grandma and Grandpa Jim,
Thank you for the shirt. I could not find anything for Grandma
Louise, but I bought myself a tee shirt which has the name of my
father's high school, New Trier, on it. I thought that everyone at
the reunion would get a kick out of it. The stock market isn't
doing too well these days but my uncles Jim (engineer) and Tom
(bank VP) think that Caterpillar is going to go up.
I had a nice time in Colorado even though it rained a lot and
fishing isn't really my sport. I went to a baseball camp which was
pretty good, and I think that I learned some useful things. Hope
to see you both soon.

Love, John

Ned's initial time at Devereux went very well. He was
assigned a behavior management specialist, who turned out to
be one of those people who clicked with Ned from the
beginning. Wayne understood him and worked hard in
helping Ned to understand the demands of his new life. In no
time he was walking across the campus to his classroom and
having successful outings with his dorm. When his three-
month probationary period was over, the decision was that,
yes, they could work with Ned. In fact, he was doing better
than expected. Ned would be staying at Devereux.
Our life had now resumed a kind of normalcy, the normalcy
we had been searching for ever since Ned's aggression began.
And we were back at Balboa that summer, back as a family.
Ned was once again cavorting in the water, jumping off Jim
White's catamaran, rowing around the island with Bill, going
off to buy a frozen banana. Our neighbors welcomed us back
and remarked on how much happier Ned was looking. Bill and
Ned walked every evening to the ferry and rode across the bay
to the Fun Zone to ride the ferris wheel. They put on so many
miles going around and around that the manager finally said to
Bill, "The rest of your vacation you and your boy ride free."
They had never had such devoted customers. Ned's behavior

specialist had given us some tips about vacation: "Give Ned a choice of food for breakfast and have him make his decision before he goes to bed. Have him pick out his clothes too. And make him stick with his choices in the morning." That worked pretty well. Everything went well, and we felt that by an incredible stroke of luck we had found the right place for Ned at last.

At Christmastime we drove to Devereux for Family Day. As we sat at a picnic table on the great field in the middle of the campus, Michael told us that the treatment team was considering a reduction of Mellaril. We couldn't have wished for better news. We had always clung to the hope that Ned could be off Mellaril. We believed that Ned's intelligence was the real key to his success and that any drug might be a hindrance to him. Besides, the possible side effects were frightening. The idea that after the holidays Devereux would be reducing Ned's medication was a cheery thought to carry home with us for Christmas vacation.

Pasadena, California
January 12, 1983

Dear Joan and Roger:

The holidays are finally over and we seem to have survived. My mother and Jim have been here a month and leave on Tuesday. They are well but the hectic pace of our family life is a bit much for them. (Me too!)

Ned was home for seventeen days and did pretty well. He enjoyed himself as long as we were going to parties and entertaining him but was not very relaxed when his time was his own. He is now 5' 4" and a real teenager.

Bill finishes shooting "M*A*S*H" (for good and all) next week, but it looks as if Fr. Mulcahy will live on in a new series called (we think) "AfterMASH," set in a V.A. hospital in Missouri. It has been sold to CBS but all contracts aren't final. I suppose it's about as sure a thing as one gets in showbiz. Meanwhile he is going to do a "Love Boat," which will take him to Mexico on a cruise ship over our twenty-fifth wedding anniversary. I'm invited too!

Much love to you all and Happy New Year,
B.

"M*A*S*H" finally drew to a close. The eleventh season wound up in the spring with a marathon two-and-a-half-hour episode, and the show went out with a bang—the highest ratings in television history.

Nineteen eighty-three was turning out to be an up and down year for Ned. The attempt to reduce his Mellaril hadn't gone well; aggression had come back with a vengeance, and the medication was upped again. This was a disappointment. Perhaps Ned would function better intellectually with no medication, but getting him to that level without jeopardizing the people who had to live and work with him was a puzzle. There were times when he would not cooperate with his school or dorm programs, and by his fifteenth birthday staff who had initially been encouraged by Ned's progress had begun to feel frustrated.

When Ned was at home, Bill and I continued to rely on the method of extinguishing bad behavior by ignoring it. That summer we had a visit from our old friends, Steve and Ronnog Seaberg. They had seen very little of Ned over the years and nothing of him since the onset of his aggressive behavior. We were worried about Ned's reaction to guests in the house, especially to people he didn't know very well, and their visit overlapped the second week of Ned's summer vacation. But they caught on to extinction at once. Although Steve is an artist, he had also been trained as an actor, and he played with Ned in a vigorous and lively manner, ignoring any gestures toward violence that came his way. He showed Ned some fancy diving in "cold Lee's pool" and chased Ned in the water. Ronnog with innate gentleness just smiled at Ned, and he didn't even try to hurt her.

In July Bill went to Washington for the installation of the "M*A*S*H" exhibit at the Smithsonian. Father Mulcahy's battered Panama was to be enshrined with such artifacts of Americana as the Model T and the *Spirit of St. Louis*. But Father Mulcahy lived on; "AfterMASH" was in production, and Bill was as busy as ever. I was busy too, preparing the first show of my silk-screen prints. Twentieth Century Fox had offered Bill a glamorous new dressing room for "AfterMASH," but he wanted to stay in his old second-story room that had been such a happy place for him during the eleven years of "M*A*S*H." It was freshly painted and newly furnished, and when my show was over, we hung it with as many framed serigraphs as we could crowd onto the walls.

Pasadena, California
August 10, 1983

Dear Grandma,

I had a very enjoyable baseball season although I thought that the All-Star team would do better. I am going to lift weights this winter and am also going to be playing in a winter league so that I can keep my skills in top shape. I have learned to windsurf and am now hooked on the sport. I am looking forward to windsurfing in Balboa.

Our hot tub is moving along very slowly but it looks like it is going to be very nice when it is finished. We have taken out a lot of the bushes around the Little House and it looks very different. We are going to plant some new bushes which will add to the look of the hot tub.

Well, hope you are feeling better and hope to see you both soon.

Love, John

Staff frustration at Devereux was becoming pretty intense. It was hard for us to understand it; Balboa went smoothly and home visits continued to go very well, especially now that we had a hot tub to offer Ned. We had been having such good luck with home visits that when Bill's parents and his brother Tom and his family were visiting us at Thanksgiving, we didn't think twice about having Ned home. Foolishly, we had forgotten that we had not trained them to be with Ned; the results were disastrous. Perhaps we were hoping they would be able to follow our example, but one of the problems with extinction is that it is so hard for most people to do. As we should have anticipated, Ned was reaching out to touch at the outset of the visit. When Bill's father rebuked him sternly, he grew much more aggressive and started pinching. Bill and I did our best to head Ned off, keep him apart, interpose ourselves, but it soon was hectic and impossible. Everyone's feelings were hurt. Tom was afraid for his little Laura. His wife Judy, alone of all the family, remembered that Ned was still Ned. She chatted to him cheerfully, disregarded his aggression, and blithely went about her business. This was exactly the right approach, but, of course, not so easy to do. Finally we took Ned back to Devereux early. I vowed this would not happen again. The mix of Ned and the rest of the family was not ever going to be simple, but until the aggression was completely over (if that day ever came), we couldn't risk it. We wouldn't deprive Ned of the chance to come home for Thanksgiving and Christmas just so we could have those ideal holidays, with family and guests, everyone around the fire, carols and good cheer. First things first.

When we drove up to Devereux to pick up Ned for Christmas vacation, things had changed greatly from the optimistic predictions of Family Day the previous year. Ned had become increasingly hurtful and was finding it impossible to obey the rules of the classroom. We had a conference with Michael and several other members of the treatment team. The staff felt that they were not providing an adequate program for Ned, and they needed advice and direction to get him back on track. They recommended that we seek out one of the several established experts in the field of autism who might be willing to become involved on a consulting basis.

As we drove home with Ned sitting in the back seat, I found myself in tears. I was trying not to overreact, but when parents are told by those in charge of their child's program, "We do not feel we are meeting your child's needs," it often signals a parting of the ways. For the first time since Ned had entered Devereux, I was anxious and upset. I wanted Devereux to be Ned's home for a long, long time. Now I had the definite feeling that his position there was shaky. And what other choices were there? As far as we knew, there still were no programs for kids like Ned, and the threat of the state hospital loomed darkly over our holidays.

We decided that we would keep Ned very busy over Christmas vacation and see what the results would be. Perhaps the Devereux schedule wasn't structured enough for Ned, and

I had already become convinced that the content of his classwork was inadequate. It was the old problem of Ned being underrated. I would go back to my Institutes materials and see what we could accomplish during vacation. I even went back to the dictated letter, this time with John as secretary, the kind of secretary who takes the gist of the dictation and improves on it.

Pasadena, California
December 30, 1983

Dear Grammy and Grandpa Jim,
This letter is being written on John's computer to thank you for the nice blue vest that you sent me. I have had a good Christmas vacation eating lots of good food, jumping on my new trampoline, and singing Christmas carols. I go back to Devereux on Friday.

Love, Ned

Pasadena, California
January 4, 1984

Dear Michael:
Here is the schedule we more or less followed during Ned's Christmas vacation. We were occasionally very far behind, but we did manage to cover most of the territory each day.

9:00-10:00 A.M.
Breakfast. (Ned unloads the dishwasher or helps cook bacon or pancakes.)
Breathing exercises (masking).
Read newspaper article to Ned while he gets ready for hot tub.
Tactile stimulation (tapping and rubbing with brush, etc.).
Vocabulary (modeling use of modifiers).

10:00-11:00 A.M.
Long session in hot tub.

Breathing exercises.
Lessons (Christmas facts, story, Christmas carols read to Ned,
material on dinosaurs, scorpions, the Olympic Games).
Vocabulary.
Tactile stimulation (splashing and tickling).

11:00 A.M.-12:00 M.
Get dressed. (Read book and show lessons to Ned as he dresses.)
Breathing exercises.
Music (Mozart, Haydn).
Vocabulary.
Ned does household task (carry out trash, carry laundry, etc.).

12:00 M.
Lunch and special activity such as McDonald's, ride on the
freeway, walk to the Arroyo.

2:00-3:00 P.M.
A demanding task such as writing, answering questions about
lessons, sitting still to listen to a book.

4:00 P.M. *on*
Second hot tub session.
Tactile.
Breathing.
Vocabulary.
Lessons.

Following tub:
Read lessons to Ned as he begins to dress.
Let him have some free time to get ready for dinner.

Dinner:
Ned sets table.
Ned helps clear after dinner.
Ned gets ready for bed.

Quiet time in living room:
Sing Christmas carols.

Play with toys.
TV.

9:00 P.M.
Bed.
Story.
Gentle tactile.

At all times throughout the day we tried to use specific words to increase Ned's vocabulary: "delicious," "enormous," "fancy," "raw," "cooked," "both." If ever Ned used a sentence where one of these new words would be appropriate, we coached him to use it. He seemed to enjoy this as a game. We also showed him these words at frequent intervals during the day.

At first Ned resisted being read to, but we found that he tolerated it better when he was busy doing something else. Throughout the two weeks he came to like sitting at the table and having materials presented to him. Writing was very difficult for him and very stressful. I kept it to a minimum. I think that Ned is upset at what he knows is a deterioration of a former ability.

The greatest triumph of the vacation occurred on the day that I made Ned sign his Christmas thank you notes. He did it and was absolutely furious with me. He boycotted dinner but kept rushing downstairs to yell, "Good writing! Good writing!" over and over again. He then proceeded to dabble his fingers in my dinner, which I could not let him do. The triumph was obviously not his agitation but the fact that he did not even attempt to aggress even though he was angry, frustrated, and highly agitated.

Although Ned made no attempt to hurt me or anyone else, he did do a lot of touching. Naturally most of this touching was inappropriate to say the least. I found that the best way to minimize it was to go toward him and hug him or kiss him or poke him playfully. I also asked him to touch me appropriately: scratch my back, tickle my foot, etc. But my greatest success was with saying (smilingly), "Act grown-up." The other problem is Ned's getting enormously hung up attempting something: walking through a door, putting on a sock. Sometimes I was able to interrupt this by saying, "One, two, three, shirt off," or, "One, two, three, run downstairs."

Ned asked to watch TV one evening and sat through the entire ballet portion of The Red Shoes. *He played alone and appropriately with a remote control battery-operated car his brother gave him for Christmas and showed him how to use.*

During the entire vacation Ned was playful and happy with only two or three sessions of whining. I felt that he showed tremendous progress since summer vacation, and although it is always exhausting to be with Ned all day, this vacation was more rewarding than any previous one. Bill was working most of the time and I obviously couldn't manage alone, and so we had the help of Harry Singleton, who worked with Ned for several years and is an old friend. There were plenty of other people around, including John's girlfriend and friends and Margarita who cleans house for us, as well as neighbors and strangers in the Arroyo. We didn't attempt any parties or restaurants but we did allow John to take Ned in his car to McDonald's. All in all I think that Ned met plenty of challenges and had a number of demands made on him.

Thank you for all your interest and concern. Happy New Year.

Barbara Christopher

Getting through the holidays so smoothly gave us hope that if we found the right consultant for Devereux, Ned could still have success there. Throughout the vacation we had been thinking about Devereux's request, and finally decided to call Dr. Edward Ritvo of UCLA, whom we had heard lecture regarding his research into autism and its biochemical foundations. Dr. Ritvo suggested that we first see his associate, B. J. Freeman, a psychologist with whom he had recently written a highly regarded book on autism. It hadn't been easy to approach UCLA again. Our experience at the Neuropsychiatric Institute there had been pretty terrible, and B. J. Freeman had been on the staff of the autism unit at the time. She had even assessed Ned. I approached her with caution, perhaps with a chip on my shoulder.

"How's Ned doing these days?" she asked cheerfully.

"Not as well as we had hoped."

"Tell me about it."

"Before I go into that, B. J., will you please tell me how you have changed in your approach to the autistic since we met you years ago?"

"Practically everything has changed in autism since those days," she said. Research was showing that it might be possible to regulate certain chemical imbalances in the autistic brain using medication; structured programs and positive behavioral methods had emerged as the best way of dealing with autistic kids; automatic hospitalizations and aversive methods were out. A lot of very dedicated people were devoting their lives to this puzzling disease. It only took a few minutes of B. J.'s warmth, charm, and intelligence to convince me that in her all autistic kids have a valuable ally and that she would be an excellent person to look at Ned's Devereux program and help us salvage it.

Pasadena, California
January 19, 1984

Dear Liz:
  The holidays are over and we are plunging into the New Year by painting the kitchen. Such projects being what they are, we find we are also redoing the floor and counter top and rebuilding the windows, etc., etc.
  Ned was home for two weeks at Xmas. It was a very successful visit. We actually did a mini-program: masking, tactile, intelligence, etc. Unfortunately things are not going quite so well at Devereux and we are afraid that we are back on the merry-go-round. We have engaged a consultant to observe Ned's day and make recommendations in hopes that something can work out. It is still the best place and most importantly he likes it. Devereux is not saying that they won't continue with Ned but only that they may not be able to do so. Another alternative is the establishment of an autism project up there, possibly an apartment for four or five autistic adolescents. That sounds hopeful but would involve us in a lot of fundraising.
  John is on the last lap of high school, and things seem to be going pretty well. He has been accepted at several colleges and will have to make the great decision. I am so ready to be the

*mother of a college student living hundreds of miles from home!
As he becomes more responsible and mature I long to have him on
his own even more.*

*Bill has only three more shows in this season; renewal is more
or less certain for a second year but as he has a new agent (this was
just to be a hasty note but I can't seem to stop) and a new press
representative, he expects to be very busy during the hiatus
(showbiz for "break between the seasons"). We have been pretty
pleased with "AfterMASH" but are hoping it will be stronger
next year with more personal life developed for Fr. Mulcahy. The
writers still have a tendency to see a priest as only priestly and
not as a man, and the priestly part is pretty cliché. This despite
lots of research and some meetings with absolutely wonderful,
real-life, entertaining, witty, vital men who are priests.*

*We long to see you and still think you should move to
California.*

Thank you for the chocolates, which I am trying not to eat.

Must stop. Love to all, B.

B. J. Freeman traveled to Devereux and spent two days
observing Ned and talking to the staff. She found that Ned was
spending a great deal of his time alone—eating alone, sitting
alone in the day room when the other kids were on outings.
She felt that the staff wanted to provide a better program for
him but were stumped by his aggressive behavior and the ups
and downs of his ability to function. Ned was not at all
aggressive toward B. J. and talked to her a little. She came away
with some concrete ideas about program and felt that Ned
would be manageable with the right approach. She and Dr.
Ritvo put their heads together, and the four of us met. Their
recommendations concerned two areas of Ned's life that
needed changing. One would be relatively easy to accomplish.
Dr. Ritvo's research at UCLA had found that low doses of
fenfluramine, a diet drug that had been on the market for a
number of years, could affect the brain chemical serotonin, and
produce improvements in a significant number of autistic
children. He agreed to consult with the physician at Devereux
on the gradual introduction of fenfluramine, accompanied by

the reduction of and eventual elimination of Mellaril. Second, they recommended a highly structured program where "every minute would be planned." Ned should have something he was supposed to be doing every single minute, and if for some reason he could not do that thing, there should be an alternate something he should be doing. Of course, we agreed wholeheartedly. Dr. Ritvo emphasized that such a program could be written by anyone with expertise, but its success depended on the people implementing it. He said that this is where most good programs break down. He recommended that we consult with Robert Koegel at the University of California at Santa Barbara, as he was much closer to Devereux and would have available a pool of excellent people who could do the actual work with Ned.

Our next step was to contact Robert Koegel. He and his staff observed Ned both at Devereux and at UCSB. The meeting at his office with Ned was an interesting adventure. Ned started out being particularly aggressive and lit into Dr. Koegel, pinching and attempting to bite.

I wasn't sure what was expected of us, but I finally said, "Do you want to handle this, or do you want us to help?"

"I don't particularly like getting hurt," he said and suggested that he and his staff retire behind the magic mirror and observe us with Ned. He was very interested in what we had found to be successful in handling Ned's aggressive behaviors.

I turned to Ned. "This is a difficult situation for us all, Ned. You are meeting a lot of new people and you are in a new place. Please try to use words instead of hurting." I hugged him and rubbed his back. Bill began talking to Ned in a soothing way and gradually calmed him down. Bill picked up some magazines and showed Ned pictures and continued chatting. Pretty soon Ned was talking, identifying objects and presenting a very different self. Dr. Koegel called me out, leaving Bill and Ned together, and in front of his staff queried me about Ned's background and how we had worked with him. He selected the staff members he thought would be able to establish rapport and control over Ned rapidly and sent them into the room, one by one. Eventually Bill left, and Alice Wyatt stayed alone with Ned and began at once to communicate with him. It was quite remarkable. Our total visit had taken only an hour and when we left, Ned kissed Alice good-bye and shook hands with everyone.

Dr. Koegel took a few days to mull over his thoughts on how Ned could be helped. As the best person to design and supervise a program he suggested one of his former students, Dr. T. J. Glahn, a psychologist with considerable experience in designing teaching-living environments for autistic children and in training staff to implement her programs. He also believed that Dr. Glahn's non-aversive approach was in accord with our personal attitude and with that of Devereux. He suggested that we use Alice Wyatt as the primary hands-on therapist, as she had already established a bond with Ned.

We were confident that the caring staff at Devereux, who had demonstrated their concern and flexibility by recommending that we bring in outside consultants, would welcome the help, that they would be willing to give such a program their all. I made an appointment for us to meet T. J. Glahn.

CHAPTER 10

Friends

Barbara and I arrived very early for our appointment with T. J. Glahn; we were eager to get on with a solution to Ned's difficulties at Devereux. T. J. was in her jogging clothes, and in a brief exchange as she stood over our heads on her small balcony, she suggested a coffee shop where we might kill a few minutes while she got ready for us. "She's a jogger," I said. "I think we're on to something."

"Yes," said Barbara. "She's also very pretty."

We smiled at each other.

After conferring all morning, T. J., Barbara, and I drove to Devereux and met Ned at his dorm. We all walked across the campus, talking as we went. Ned lagged behind and kept kneeling down to pick up leaves and shred them. "We'll have to do something about that behavior," T. J. said, "but for now, let's join Ned on the grass." We all sat, and T. J. talked to Ned gently, patting him on the back and taking his hand. And although Ned didn't respond in words, he was relaxed and did not attempt to pinch. By the time we had spent half an hour together, it was clear to us that T. J. had a feeling for Ned. We talked more about Ned's history, particularly emphasizing the success of his Institutes intelligence program. T. J. was cautious, and I could see that she didn't quite believe we were correct in our assessment of Ned's intelligence. But when we arrived back at the dorm, Barbara and Ned gave a demonstration using Ned's old Institutes materials, and although it had been two and a half years since his home program, Ned remembered everything. In all the questions Barbara put to him that day, he only got one wrong. T. J. was impressed. So was I.

We thought we were off to a good start. We desperately wanted Ned to stay at Devereux. That morning as we were driving onto the campus, I felt more strongly than ever that Devereux was where Ned's future lay. Perhaps the beauty of the setting gave me confidence, the buildings far apart with lots of open space, the closeness of the ocean, the air so clean and fresh. Even if his program had some holes in it, he was happy here and that meant a lot to us. I believed in the Devereux Foundation's commitment to Ned and kids like him. At an earlier time maybe Devereux would have turned down the challenge of working with such difficult clients, but times had changed. Throughout the country many people who would formerly have been in residential special schools were now living at home or in community-based group homes; those who would formerly have been in hospitals were now seeking residential placement. This meant an increasingly difficult population needing treatment at schools like Devereux. Recognizing this, the new president of the Devereux Foundation, Ron Burd, had articulated Devereux's mission of meeting this need.

Remarkably soon, Ned had a new life. T. J. immediately set up a new daily routine. She trained existing Devereux staff in new approaches and brought in a number of new people to work with Ned. Naturally, there were some resentments among the Devereux staff. Those who had been working with Ned for the past year and a half didn't much like an outsider coming in to take over. But we decided that we could not allow ourselves to focus on hurt feelings. That could not be our problem, or Ned's. We were trying to save his life, for that is how we saw it. We all had to give a little. We, of course, had to bow to T. J.'s expertise. T. J. had to put up with us, demanding parents who had very definite ideas about what was good for their son. Ned had to get used to another way of life. It was an interesting period.

From the beginning, of course, attention had to be focused on Ned's behavior, specifically on his aggression. But since behavior doesn't exist in a vacuum, an important consideration was the content of his days.

Ned's academics included writing, coin discrimination, telling time, reading, math, and use of his Institutes materials for general education. The goal of this new academic program was eventual integration into a regular Devereux classroom, but for the time being Ned worked alone with his special staff. He had a language development program organized and supervised by the Devereux speech therapist.

Ned had very specific programs in many other areas:

Hair Brushing:
1. Pick up brush with right hand.
2. Starting at crown, brush forward through hair on top of head five times.
3. Starting at crown, brush down through hair on back of head five times.
4. Starting at crown, brush down through hair on right side of head five times.
5. Reach across head and starting at crown, brush down through hair on opposite side of head five times.
6. Put brush down.

Each time Ned brushed his hair, he was talked through this procedure, and slowly the directions faded away as he moved toward the goal of complete independence. He had similar programs in meal preparation, showering, toothbrushing, shaving, bed making, room cleaning, crossing the street, and table manners.

I had never thought of myself as lax in the area of table manners, but I began to see the possibility of improvement. Perhaps when T. J. got Ned fixed, she could turn her methods on the rest of us. T. J. reevaluated and updated her strategies weekly, and she revised the overall plan regularly.

Ned's highly structured program extended into what had been leisure activities. It was simply true that Ned did not do very well in managing his own time. He was better at working than playing. But now he had programs in exercise, listening to music, operating a cassette player, playing catch. He also had frequent forays into the community with exposure to recreational facilities, restaurants, museums.

Alice Wyatt had joined T. J.'s team, and she and Lorraine Lim, who had a great deal of experience working with aggressive people, were now Ned's principal companions. We first glimpsed Lorraine as she walked toward us across the campus central field, hand-in-hand with Ned. From a distance it looked as if Ned must be in charge of Lorraine, for she only came up to his shoulder. She had a jaunty walk and an enthusiastic manner, and I knew the minute I saw them together that she was already a favorite with our son.

Ned was busy all day long. The intensity of his program and all the one-to-one attention created the bond he needed; his therapists had become his friends. Now when Ned came home for visits, he was accompanied by one of his "friends," and we noticed something new in him. As we sat at our round kitchen table, he turned his body toward Lorraine, T. J., Alice, shouldering us out. Like any other teenager, he wanted his friends to himself. I thought it was quite an accomplishment for the therapists to maintain authority and still create the bond of friendship, but of course they had youth on their side. The difficulty of forming friendships for an autistic child is a sad thing to observe. Now all of a sudden Ned really had friends. True, they were not his peers, but perhaps that would come later. T. J. was sure it would. We felt encouraged that Ned had made this step toward relationships with people outside the tiny group he had been familiar with most of his life. As T. J. had access to a pool of students from UCSB, she was able to continue Ned's program throughout the weekend using them as trainee-therapists—or trainee-therapist-friends.

At first Ned reacted to all these challenges with serious aggression. As soon as anyone tried to make demands on him, or even give him simple directions, aggression was quick to begin and quick to escalate. It was important for Ned as well as for his therapist-buddies that no one get hurt. T. J. dealt with this by putting ski-gloves on Ned, rendering his pinches less hurtful. To protect themselves further, the staff wore down-filled vests. Before the gloves were introduced, Ned was shown reading cards outlining exactly what the gloves were for and under what conditions he would be allowed to take them off. Ned was at once less aggressive; he even put the gloves on willingly, and although he could remove them if he really tried, he left them on perhaps as a reminder to himself.

By the time June arrived, our optimism and confidence had returned in full force. Ned was continuing to improve. John, who had just graduated from high school, had managed to line up a job working for the Olympic Games, which were coming to Los Angeles that summer; I pulled off a magnificent surprise party for Barbara's birthday; and we all set off for Balboa in high spirits. This is how Ned's improvement struck our Grand Canal neighbor:

> Balboa Island
> August 1, 1984

Dear Barbara and Bill:

It has come into my mind that I made a friend when you were here this summer. As I walked in from the dock, Ned was on the seawall and Bill was on the sidewalk. I walked along and said, "Hi, Ned." He quickly answered and said, "Hi," and shook my hand. Then he said again, "Hi," and shook my hand again. I felt he had overcome a great deal and indeed we are friends. Ned, you made my day, week, month. See you next year.

Jim White

PS Frozen bananas are alive and well.

At the Regional Center meeting to review Ned's program, the counselor was equally impressed with Ned's growth and improvement:

> Autistic behaviors coming more under control and are less of a barrier to program. Great progress over last quarter. Aggression, knee-dropping, stim decreased. Marked improvement in socialization.

At the end of the summer, we drove John to college and stopped off en route to see Ned. It was a milestone, and we wanted Ned to be in on it. Barbara and I were going to be alone in our house for the first time in eighteen years!

San Francisco, California
September 3, 1984

Dear Dad, Mom & Ned,
Here is the first of those treasured letters. I hope everyone is fine. I just started classes two days ago and they seem all right. I'm taking math, U.S. history, philosophy, and sociology. They all seem rather interesting although I've only had one class in each. I don't have much class time but do have a good amount of homework.
Bad news—my computer won't go on. I think it's the power source again.

Love, John

With shooting completed on the first nine scripts, "After-MASH" took a break, and Barbara and I celebrated our new independence by taking a vacation in France. We drove through the countryside and were staying at the wonderful Colombe d'Or in St. Paul de Vence when the call came from my agent. The show had been canceled. I can't pretend that I wasn't very disappointed, but looking out over the rugged hills above Nice, dining every evening in a room hung with Picassos, Legers, Calders, it was impossible to feel that I was anything but a very lucky fellow. And perhaps it was time for Father Mulcahy to hang up his gloves.

On our desk amid the stacks of mail waiting for us when we came home was a note from Devereux enclosing a remarkable snapshot of Ned dressed in a white gown with giant wings on his back. Brenda, one of T. J.'s students who had been working with Ned on weekends, had made Ned a lovely costume for Halloween and had taken him to the Devereux all-campus Halloween party. His appearance as an angel was, we hoped, symbolic of the improvement in his behavior.

"If you go about it systematically and with enthusiasm, the most marvelous things happen," said T. J., and we agreed. As we read her monthly reports, we saw the data on Ned's behavior grow more and more encouraging. We felt confident that Ned had an excellent and highly enriched program. We watched Ned's improvement in behavior, skills, and happiness, and began to envision the possibility of a program at Devereux especially geared to the needs of autistic kids, the kind of autistic kids who were very difficult to place. Perhaps T. J.'s work with Ned could be the basis of such an autism program. And how this could be accomplished was a question I began to puzzle over. I had recently become a member of Devereux's national board, and as a trustee I felt a certain responsibility to share my thoughts with the president of the foundation.

Pasadena, California
December 6, 1984

Mr. Ronald P. Burd, President
The Devereux Foundation
19 South Waterloo Road
Devon, Pennsylvania 19333

Dear Ron:
Thank you for following up on the progress of Ned's program at Devereux in Santa Barbara. I would like to stress that I am very aware of the dedication of the staff to their responsibilities toward Ned. My interest, however, in taking up the matter with you in Philadelphia was to see where we might be able to go in building on Ned's program to establish a pilot project for autistic adolescents and young adults at Santa Barbara.

The excellent progress that Ned has made since Dr. T. J. Glahn was taken on as a consultant has made us very eager to see this kind of program enlarged to include other kids. What I envision is a comprehensive program taking advantage of the strides in educating the autistic that have been made in the past few years and providing the kind of highly structured, detailed program that has benefited Ned so much.

As I see it, the cornerstone of such a program is a permanent position, a psychologist or teacher with expertise in the disease who would design and direct the project. This person would train the staff in the most effective techniques for behavior management as well as education (both academic and practical) and provide each client with a highly individualized program and the kind of minute-to-minute structuring that seems to be the key to making the most of the considerable potential of these kids.

We have made an excellent beginning. The program is there but just for Ned. The burning question is where do we go from here to enlarge the program to include others, to build on the success of what is already in place, and to see Devereux take an important step in providing a much-needed service in California.

As you stated in the "President's Letter" of October, the Devereux Foundation must expect to provide services for the more seriously afflicted. A comprehensive autism project at Santa Barbara seems to fit in with that policy and to carry on the goals of this great foundation.

Very truly yours,
Bill Christopher

Ned was home for a week at Christmas, and all went well. I was working hard learning lines. For the first time in years I had been able to accept a play out of town, and shortly after the holidays I took off for Canada and a dinner theater engagement. I was to perform in a marvelous farce about a man with two wives. That was about as far from Mulcahy as I could hope to get. I loved the idea. One of the wives was called Barbara, and my own Barbara took that in stride.

Edmonton, Alberta
January 11, 1985

Dear Barbara,

Well here I am and there you are. Seems to me the last time I wrote, I had gone to New Jersey to do that hospital safety film for the Signal Corps. I suppose that was around 1966.

Can't tell you what a relief it is to be running the play through. I wish you could have been here to help with wardrobe selection, but I can't worry about that now. There are still quite a number of rather important details to be cleaned up, so they will get all my attention. You'll like the cast pretty well. All make their parts work more or less, and the balance is really tipped in favor of the more.

I'm not going on now. I love you very much, and I miss you.
By the time you read this, a lot will have happened.

Bill

The play opened in Calgary, and Barbara joined me. We had a lovely time. It was terribly cold, but we had a cozy apartment, and we enjoyed the freedom from responsibility that our situation created. No house, no dog, no garden, no kids, no friends, no social engagements. We didn't even have to make our own bed. One remarkable weekend we drove up to Banff and swam in an outdoor, naturally heated pool in a snowstorm. In order to fill the hours when I was at the theater, Barbara rented a typewriter and began a project that had been brewing in her mind for some time. It was absolutely wonderful to have this chance to do some things we had both been wanting to do for years. I was back on stage, and Barbara was writing a play, a dramatization of Jane Austen—very theatrical and unusual. Each evening when I returned from the theater, Barbara read me a new scene, and we blocked out the action on the huge coffee table in the living room. It was a great change for us, this starting over on our own life.

The wonderful and relaxed time in Canada was possible because of the confidence we felt in Ned's well-being. His progress and achievement contributed to our sense of freedom. But we returned to a much different situation. While we were away, Ned had begun to hit himself on the side of the head, a behavior that had everyone worried. Right after our return, he came home for a weekend and while he was with us, he didn't hit himself at all. But the next time we saw him, he was black and blue on both sides of his face. Staff told us that the blows he gave himself were rather infrequent but of great intensity, and judging from the bruises, we could believe it. Devereux applied to the state of California for permission to use pneumatic splints on his arms to protect Ned from himself, but that application was turned down. Another home visit, this one marking his seventeenth birthday, and still we didn't see the behavior. Yet we were getting regular reports from Devereux that Ned's head-hitting was getting in the way of everything. All the gains he had made in the past year were disappearing, and the wonderful people who worked with him were terribly upset. They had a great deal of love and effort invested in Ned. To see him hit himself, and to see him become very aggressive when anyone tried to stop him, was discouraging to them all.

It was not until our annual stay at Balboa that Barbara and I saw what they were trying to tell us. T. J. and Lorraine were with us and things started out pretty well; but toward the end of our first week there, while we were downstairs and Ned was changing into his bathing suit, we heard a terrible thumping. I ran up the stairs and into his room. He stared at me with a glazed look as he repeatedly struck himself. There was no glimmer of recognition in his eyes. His body was covered with sweat, and when I placed my hand on the side of his head to protect him from his own violence, I felt the terrible force of his blows. I seized his swinging arm and he turned on me. He saw me then, I guess, but his eyes were still glazed and wild. He scratched and bit me ferociously. T. J. and Lorraine came pelting up the stairs and caught Ned in their expert grips. As he was being restrained, T. J. gave him calm and soothing directions, reassuring him in a kindly way. In a few minutes the tension went out of Ned's body. They gradually released him and immediately began to work with him at the table, showing him bits of information, engaging his intelligence in a battle to overcome this strange impetus to hurt himself. In the past, whenever Ned had been aggressive, he had been aware of his actions; most of the time he had been penitent. But this time he appeared to have no memory at all of what had happened.

As planned, Ned returned to Devereux for the weekend and came back to Balboa with Alice on Tuesday. During this second stay we felt as if we were sitting on an unexploded bomb. And on Thursday evening the bomb went off. Barbara, Ned, Alice, and I had taken the ferry across the bay to the Fun Zone to ride the ferris wheel, something we had done every night of the vacation. Ned was tense and irritable, and when we reached the other side, he started to run about reaching out at strangers. I tried to head him off, interposing my body between him and anybody else, but it was not an easy task. I could see his hostility growing as well as his determination. I turned to Barbara: "Let's get out of here! Now!"

We headed for the ferry and boarded. Ned continued to reach out toward those around him. He hadn't actually laid hands on anyone, but there was an ever-present danger, and the ferry was crowded. There was no choice but to take a seat on the side benches, facing the cars. Alice and I sat with Ned between us, attempting to keep him corralled. He was crying loudly and tearlessly and was very agitated. The trip, only about three minutes long, seemed like an Atlantic crossing. Ned kept trying to reach around us, constantly jumping up from his place and sitting down again. Naturally everyone in the cars and all the pedestrian passengers had their eyes glued on us. Something was going on, and they couldn't quite tell what.

Barbara walked along the ranks of passengers explaining our predicament: "We have our autistic son with us, and he is having an aggressive episode. It would help us very much if you would not look at him or pay any attention at all to his behavior. And please stay away from him. We don't want anyone to get hurt. When we get off the ferry, we might have to restrain him, but we won't be hurting him." She moved along to another group of passengers: "We have our autistic son with us . . ."

Both Alice and I knew that if Ned did grab onto anyone, we would have to pull him away by force. If that happened, Ned would very likely turn into a biting, scratching, kicking animal. He was small for seventeen, but he was very strong. So we were jumping up and down with him, talking to him, trying to keep his attention. Unfortunately, just before the ferry docked, Ned would not be contained any longer. He grabbed an arm sticking out of a car window, and I had to lay hold of him. That was all it took. We had a real battle on our hands. Somehow we managed to get Ned, fighting and struggling, off the ferry and into a dingy corner near the public restrooms. There we got him down on the ground and restrained him. One of the passengers came to our aid. I was startled to see him kneeling next to me holding an arm, but he apparently knew what he was doing.

"You look as if you've done this before."

"Yes," he said, "I've had some training."

"Glad you could be here," I said. "No, don't let go as soon as he relaxes, you might get hurt. We go through some counting. That seems to help."

A lifeguard who had been on the ferry stood with great authority and told people to keep moving, reassuring them that everything was all right, while Barbara ran as fast as she could back to the house for medication, Ned's gloves, and the car. Once on, the gloves worked their spell, reminding Ned that he should not hurt people. The episode was about over, and as he grew calmer, we thanked our kind helper and told him that we could manage without him now. Just as we were beginning to release Ned and get him on his feet, a passerby approached me. "Hey, Father! Can I have your autograph?"

The last day of the vacation went well enough, but we were scared. This level of behavior was beyond anything we had seen, and we weren't sure what help there was for it. After all, we had always maintained that a good, complete program was the answer. We knew that Devereux would not be able to keep Ned much longer if these explosive fits could not be brought under control.

In July we had the great good luck to attend the annual conference of the Autism Society of America (at that time called the National Society for Autistic Children and Adults), which was held in Los Angeles that year. Devereux sent Lorraine and Gary White, another of the outstanding staff members, and we all sat fascinated as we heard a professor from Harvard Medical School discuss the first autopsy studies of an autistic person's brain. Ed Ritvo and B. J. Freeman presented their current work on genetic studies in autism. We saw a remarkable demonstration by the students and staff of Kiyo Kitahara's school in Tokyo, a school where several hundred autistic kids are integrated into four times as many normal kids, in a program that is very physical and in which, we were told, the body teaches the brain. (That sounded familiar.) We were terribly impressed with the students who had traveled all the way from Japan to show us their remarkable achievements, and with the expertise and energy of the staff working with them. Then Dr. Paul Hardy from Massachusetts presented a moving lecture about seriously self-injurious kids who had been helped with medication to prevent panic-anxiety disorder, which had everyone in the audience in tears. Some things he said struck both Barbara and me as descriptive of Ned's attacks on himself. We talked to Dr. Hardy later in the day, and he said that rather than panic-anxiety attacks, it sounded to him as if Ned might be having temporal lobe seizures. He offered to discuss his ideas with the physician at Devereux.

Dr. Hardy was as good as his word, and very soon Devereux started Ned on a trial period of Tegretol. Miraculously, the self-injurious behavior disappeared—immediately! Reluctant as we were to have Ned on another medication, this one seemed necessary. However, the months of disruption of Ned's routine, his increased aggression and agitation, and the discouragement of the staff dealing with him during the long period of self-injury had taken its toll on his program and on Ned. It was almost impossible to believe it, but the great improvement that had occurred had now disappeared. Once more Ned was spending most of his time challenging his therapists with pinches and refusing to participate in his lessons. He had developed the habit of attempting to mouth the hands of anyone working with him. All in all Ned managed to avoid having any content in his day. He wasn't hitting himself; for that we were grateful, but we began to despair that he would ever get back to the level of programming that he needed to be at his best. The staff were struggling along but morale was low.

Then someone else entered our lives and Ned's. Tom McCool came to Devereux that September as director of programs. He had years of experience in special education as a teacher and as an administrator, and Devereux began at once under his direction to get Ned moving forward again. It had been demonstrated that Ned could do well and that he could do well in the setting at Devereux; the interruption in his program caused by his bizarre self-injury was over; now it was urgent to get him and his program back on track. Tom provided the ingredient that had been missing up to this time, an administrator committed to the kind of program that we had been trying to ensure for Ned. It isn't enough to have dedicated and capable people to design and execute a program; to achieve a good program that will survive the ups and downs of an autistic child and the comings and goings of available staff, it is necessary to have an administrator involved to provide leadership and support. Tom had three sons of his own and encountered our parental frustration and impatience with understanding and relaxed confidence. Now we began to work closely not only with the therapists but with the administrator who was responsible for the program.

Pasadena, California
October 7, 1985

Dear Tom:

Thank you for your letter, notes from the planning meeting, and memo to the staff. These documents as well as our phone conversations make it clear that Ned's new program is off to a solid start.

We appreciate your invitation to give our input into the process of developing activities that will implement Ned's IEP. Perhaps we can get together soon to discuss in detail some of the educational methods we have used with Ned at home with success.

We look forward to seeing you at the Devereux event on Thursday evening.

Very truly yours,
Barbara and Bill Christopher

We were full of ideas, and as we passed them on to Tom McCool, we were constantly thinking of how our approaches for Ned could be beneficial to many kids like him. As Tom continued to be receptive, we continued to put our ideas on paper.

Pasadena, California
November 1, 1985

Dear Tom:
Following our stimulating discussion on Monday, we began to wonder about how we would like to see a day structured.

The enclosed is the result of our thinking. I realize that it does not reflect any knowledge of staffing or other logistic problems that may exist. This hypothetical schedule also reflects our personal bent toward plenty of physical exercise, tactile input, and a high degree of structure. It is loosely based, as you can tell, on the way we worked with Ned.

Having thought this out I have decided to send it on to you. It would be interesting to see how others would imagine developing a schedule and content in order to accomplish the goals.

Sincerely,
Barbara Christopher

On receiving this letter, accompanied by Barbara's ten-page outline of our ideas, Tom probably felt he had a tiger by the tail. But we felt a great need to get something done and get it done now! If Tom was at all puzzled by the flood of response thrown at him from the general direction of Pasadena, he didn't show it. He suggested that Barbara do a videotaped demonstration of the Institutes method of increasing intelligence that had been so successful with Ned. The tape could be used as a training tool for staff.

Pasadena, California
November 20, 1985

Dear Steve and Ronnog:
It was so wonderful to see you in Atlanta. We returned home and plunged right in at Devereux with a meeting yesterday in which I demonstrated the use of the Institutes educational materials with Ned. He showed off wonderfully (me too!). He was able to answer all but one of the questions I asked him in a forty-minute session. They videotaped the session, and that made me quite nervous. (How odd to feel nervous doing something I have done thousands of times, but the presence of the camera has a strange power.) The staff (who have been skeptical to say the least) now want me to have weekly meetings to teach this method. Naturally I am very pleased at this reception.

Our efforts are having an impact on Ned's life, but we are a long way from the complete autism program that we would like to see. It should not be this difficult for handicapped people to get what they need! Ned seemed great to us, but reports are that his behavior is up and down. We are hoping for an up period over Thanksgiving.

John says he is enjoying college, but whether he is doing anything more than enjoying, we aren't sure.

Love from us, B.

In taking charge of Ned's program, Tom involved more Devereux staff and surveyed them on their ideas about programming. In order to develop a more comprehensive autism program and expand the project to include more kids, Tom felt that he needed a full-time coordinator. T. J.'s role now became that of consultant to Devereux for staff training. Early in the new year the coordinator was hired, and we began the difficult process of trying to convince yet another professional that Ned was capable of learning. A new autism classroom was established, and a teacher and psychologist were assigned to the program. Communication with the new team was made somewhat harder as I had accepted a job playing in *The Seven Year Itch* in the Washington, D.C., area. In spite of the ease of telephones and the possibility of writing letters (an opportunity I avail myself of all too rarely), there is nothing like face-to-face talking to really communicate. Well, we would have to put up with the distance. We felt confident that Ned was in good hands.

Indeed, communication worked fairly well. The new autism coordinator sent us a comprehensive plan for Ned's program for our perusal while we were away. When we returned to California, there were countless meetings to discuss the objectives for Ned and for the autism project.

As a first step, Ned moved into a new dorm where his life was merged with that of other boys. The special staff who had been working with Ned for so long had found it a great strain. Now Ned would learn to share those therapists who had been "his" with other kids, and he would learn to work with many new people. These were great challenges for Ned, as he had to work out his relationship with each new person. He usually did this by testing their reactions to his pinches. But on the whole, the transition was somewhat easier than everyone anticipated, and soon Ned was no longer wearing gloves. Ned liked Beta, his new dorm, so much that when he came home for a visit and it was time to drive back to Devereux, he cried, "No go to Devereux." What was going on, we wondered? Ned had always returned to Devereux quite willingly. This mystery was solved when en route I mentioned Beta. "Go to Beta," Ned said happily. So that was it. He thought that Devereux was the name of his old dorm; he was delighted to be going back to Beta.

In July Tom and the autism treatment team traveled to Washington, D.C., for the annual Autism Society conference. So did Barbara. I had to miss it as I was busy doing another play, this time in North Carolina. But Barbara called me each evening from the conference with excited reports. And John called me each evening from home with details of a water-heater crisis. With his new maturity he was coping splendidly—plumbers and appointments and water everywhere.

I was especially sorry to miss that conference. Every year just a little more is known about this very baffling disease. At least one of us had attended, and Barbara wrote to some of the other Devereux parents who shared our interest in autism.

Pasadena, California
July 22, 1986

Dear Friends:
I have just returned from the national Autism Society Conference and thought I would share my impressions with you. Tom McCool and the treatment team also attended, but (due to the organization of the conference—very little program content and plenty of time to talk in the first two days, and too much content and no time to talk during the second two days) I have not heard their impressions of the meetings.
First of all, one of the themes that seems to be emerging is the

division of autistic persons into subgroups; as Mary Coleman (a leading biologist in the study of autism) stated in the closing address of the conference, "Autism is no longer a diagnosis, it is a description." The main significance of these subgroups is for research leading (with luck) to specific medications and specific strategies for remediation through education and training. At the present, however, as far as this conference went, the discussions resolved into "high functioning" (meaning verbal, main-streamed in school and community, high IQ) and "lower functioning" (meaning mentally retarded). There was very little attention paid to the issues that I know from our discussions at our house a few weeks ago are important to all of us, i.e., the growth of the whole person regardless of his functional level. This impression may be due to the selections I made, but it did seem to me that many issues specific to my child were not addressed. I also do not like to hear function equated with independence. There is certainly a kind of function that needs a great deal of support and stimulation.

One of the most thrilling experiences for me was to hear Temple Grandin speak. She is a woman in her thirties who was severely autistic in early childhood and who has recovered to the extent that she has a job in the cattle industry and is currently getting her doctorate. She has written a book on her experiences growing up called Emergence: Labeled Autistic. She was scheduled to speak for forty-five minutes, but the interest of both parents and professionals kept her at it all morning on the closing day of the conference. Of particular interest to me was her discussion of the importance of sensory therapy for the autistic as part of a program including education and also medication. It is her feeling that professionals tend to get hooked in one area or another and that autistic people need a range of programs to meet their needs. She spoke movingly of the terrible dilemma of having to choose to let in all of the sensory stimuli, which was like "having a freight train" going through her head, or to shut it all out and isolate herself. She praised her speech therapist who helped her to develop language to a normal level and her teacher who instead of attempting to redirect her fixation (with cattle-moving equipment) taught her to use it (her career in the *livestock business). I can hardly capsulize what it took her hours to say, but it isn't necessary—she has written a book. It was, however, incredible to be really talking to someone who knows what it is like to be autistic and who has the skills and intelligence to explain it to us.*

Barbara Christopher

Ned had benefited from sensory integration years ago, and now we discovered that Mike Babcock, one of the occupational therapists already on staff at Devereux, was trained in sensory integration procedures. He enthusiastically threw himself into designing activities that might help Ned. A sensory integration room was set up, and lots of tactile stimulation and motor activities were reintroduced into Ned's life. One more program element was in place for Ned.

Another important step was taken. A new attempt was made to lower Ned's Mellaril, this time very, very slowly. Previous efforts had been unsuccessful, and we waited rather apprehensively for the reports from Devereux. As before there was some increase in aggression and agitation, but Glenn Miller, the new medical director, was convinced that it was important for Ned's overall well-being to get him off this drug. He predicted that Ned's behavior would improve as his body adjusted to each lowered dosage, and he emphasized the importance of a strong program to support the behavioral goals as the medication levels were reduced. He reassured us and the staff that Ned's intelligence would be more available to him on less Mellaril and that should make behavior strategies more effective. As he adjusted to each change, Ned's behavior stabilized, and he became more alert and happier. Slowly throughout the year Ned's Mellaril dose would grow smaller and smaller.

Ned's teacher kept him busy with academics and plenty of physical activity. He was back to regular running, first around the campus and later along what came to be called the beach route. And he was learning to type. Coached at the typewriter,

Ned let us know what he would like to eat on his next home visit.

2-3-87

Ned's list of things to eat at home:

1.waffles
2.corn
3.spaghetti
4.hot dogs

It was great to get a typewritten message from Ned. The typing was somewhat dim and irregular, and I knew the effort it must have taken. But if he could manage that, I would somehow find him corn in February. I found some—tough, out-of-season corn, but Ned loved it.

Things did not always go smoothly. Home visits became especially difficult when Ned developed two new behaviors. He had begun to tear his clothing and to enjoy breaking dishes, or breaking anything that would hit the floor with a fine crash. We had always prided ourselves on having an attractive house with lots of objects around, despite having an autistic child. We were sure that long familiarity with a normal home would be good for him and never dreamt that he might begin to enjoy taking it apart. Were things never going to settle down? Probably not. Ned-proofing became a new routine. After all, Ned still wanted his home visits, and we wanted him home.

May 22, 1987

Dear Mom and Dad:
　Hi. I miss you. When are you coming to see me? When am I coming home to visit? Call me or write to me soon.

Love, Ned

Although the autism program was going forward, it was happening too slowly for us. Nothing ever happens fast enough for parents who are thinking continually of the passage of time, of their children growing up. As always with the formation of new programs, there were difficulties to be surmounted, a certain amount of trial and error. The original coordinator decided instead on a career in research at UCSB, and as part of his new work reentered Ned's life as a one-to-one tutor in an experimental cooking program. Kathleen Kinkela, Ned's teacher, became the coordinator, another teacher was hired, and a committee of parents and staff was formed to observe and report on successful existing programs, to contact respected leaders in the field of autism for their input, and to hash out some of the financial and philosophical problems that every new program encounters.

Ned, of course, was not standing still waiting for the perfect program, the perfect facility, the perfect staff-student ratio, or the perfect philosophy. He had to get on with his everyday life. Linda, Ned's new teacher, thought he needed some new interests. So many aspects of Ned's life had been around for years, we all thought he must be bored with them without quite realizing it. Now he was learning to cook, learning to ride a bike, enrolled in a horse riding program, and learning to use the telephone.

At the end of 1987 I accepted another theater job, this time in Kansas City, and for the first time we would not be with our kids for Christmas. For a normal child, a normal family, this is hard enough, but for us it was particularly hard. Betty and Jim were in Pasadena to get away from the winter weather and to be with John for the holidays. But what about Ned? Did Ned realize why he wasn't going home for Christmas? Did he know that the packages he received from Kansas City were from us? Did he understand that we would be back to see him soon?

The phone rang in our Kansas City apartment and I answered it.

"Hello?"

"Hi, this is Stan, calling from the classroom. Ned is ready to talk to you."

"Hi, Ned."

Silence.

"Hi, Ned," I whispered this time.

"Hi, Daddy," came a faint whisper.

"Happy New Year, Ned."

"Happy New Year," very faintly.
"I love you, Ned. I miss you."
Silence.
"Did you get the shoes we sent you?"
"Shoes."
"Great, Ned. You got the shoes. Are you wearing them?"
"Shoes."
"Great, Ned. We will be home soon."
"Good-bye, Daddy."

Barbara picked up the extension.
"Hi, Ned."
"Hi, Mommy."
"Did you have a nice Christmas?"
"Green apple."
"I'll be back home next week, and I'll bring you a green apple."
"Good-bye, Mommy."
"I love you, Ned."
The faintest of whispers, "I love you."

Hearing Ned's voice and Stan's, we felt at ease. Ned was with his friends.

CHAPTER 11

Dreams

A Dream for America!

I have a brother who has a problem with his brain. My brother, Ned, does not play normally. Ned likes to throw leaves, run back and forth and very carefully make layouts with some plastic letters and small blocks.

Sometimes, when he gets excited, he laughs and jumps up and down.

Often, Ned (when he's in bed) gets on his hands and knees and rocks back and forth.

Ned has problems in expressing what he wants in the correct words.

Strangely enough, when he was two years old he knew the names of many flags like Czechoslovakia and Yugoslavia which he still knows.

Personally, I think Ned has in the last year increased in stating what he wants. But Ned has decreased in that he used to be able to read words like TIN, FIN, PIN, etc.

Ned was born with this problem and I don't think he will ever come very close to beating it.

Ned's problem many other children have (except they do different things) and my dream is sort of obvious.

An essay written by John Christopher
at age ten, on Martin Luther King Day

One of the greatest fears that plagues the parents of a handicapped child is what will happen when they are no longer there to fight his battles? Who will stand up for him, who will care? There's John, of course, a loving brother, but that is a heavy legacy. There was the time John cried, "Why can't I have a real brother?" Why not, indeed? And can the love that John has always had for Ned survive the realities of responsibility for an autistic person? There is Devereux, an excellent and caring organization that is well established and determined to provide good programs, but the survival of such institutions depends on the supply of good people to run them and on the adequacy of funding, public and private. The only sound insurance for kids like Ned is a better world. And like John's dream at age ten, our dreams are sort of obvious. Sometimes they are general, encompassing a great improvement in society so that it will come to value every person, irrespective of his productivity (as if there were no other values in human life). In these dreams the professions are peopled with great thinkers willing to devote their lives to unpopular diseases, the legislatures, with men and women of compassion and vision; educators care about true education—a leading out of the darkness; we have a president and governors who care enough to learn about the handicapped and to serve them as well as their more visible constituents; we have government agencies that put adequate money into research toward the prevention and cure of all forms of disability; clinicians use their full creative powers instead of relying on old, worn-out approaches; therapists are never satisfied; the brave and loyal people who give their lives to the service of the handicapped are highly paid and highly valued; professionals of every stamp set aside their petty jealousies and work toward their common goals; and parents never give up.

John, when he was a little boy, said to us once, "Wouldn't it be funny if Ned suddenly started to talk like a normal kid, if we found out that he has been fooling us all the time?" That dream is one we have all had—those of us who know Ned and have seen his flashes of brilliance.

We have other dreams for Ned, too, sometimes very simple dreams. In these dreams Ned walks toward us. He looks handsome and healthy, as he always does. But when we greet him, he begins to talk, freed of the bonds of his disease; he is free of random movements, free of the confusion and pain that surround him much of the time. In these dreams he grows up and has the pains and pleasures of a normal person; he marries and has kids of his own to dream about and to worry about; he drives a car and has a job and makes his own decisions.

But for the most part we confine our dreams to the realities that we can try to affect. The autism committee meets, and we continue our discussion of ideas for a model project: a comprehensive twenty-four-hour-a-day program with a highly trained staff helping a small group of young autistic adults (yes, Ned is an adult, although it is hard for us to think of him as such) to manage their own lives. There would be plenty of contact with the community, vocational and educational goals, involvement with non-handicapped peers. Others on the committee have their ideas, but ours as usual include lots of physical activity and regular exposure to high-level intellectual and cultural material. There will be more meetings to begin to shape this raw dream material into an actual, excellent program. We know, of course, that when this excellent program exists, we will go on wanting more, that we will never be satisfied, that we will keep on dreaming.

The committee meeting is over, and we stroll across the grounds to Ned's classroom. The class is just leaving, and we pile into the van and pull out of the campus driveway. Linda is behind the wheel. Ned is in the very last seat in the van, his favorite. We head for the horseback exercise and riding program that the 4H provides for handicapped kids. Ned is very excited. He can't resist unbuckling his seat belt, and at each unbuckling Linda pulls over, and we wait for Ned to obey that prime rule of the school van. Everyone stays calm, and eventually we pull up next to the corral. Stan, Linda's aide, gets out with Ned, and we sit almost breathless waiting to see what will happen. Ned knows his way around here. He marches into the shed and reappears wearing a helmet. Safety again. "Perhaps we should prepare him some lessons on the history of safety equipment." "Good idea," says Linda. "Now just watch this." The 4H instructor joins Ned and Stan and hands Ned a rope. After a bit of preliminary skirmishing in which Ned reaches out toward the instructor and she proves herself a real professional by keeping him focused on the task at hand, the three of them enter the corral. In a minute or two Ned reappears, holding the rope and striding out purposefully, leading the horse. The expression on his face is one of pride, and every so often a little smile flickers across his lips. The horse, Frosty, is twenty years old, just about Ned's age. He isn't of overwhelming size, just a nice, medium-sized horse and very, very gentle and patient. Ned and Frosty are well matched in their pace, both having long, slim legs. With Stan's gentle coaxing Ned leads Frosty into the ring. For half an hour Ned leads Frosty about, occasionally stopping to bury his face in Frosty's coat. Then both boy and horse take the next step in this program. Ned puts the blanket and saddle on Frosty's back and once again leads him around. That's enough for today. Next week Ned will try to get up on the horse. We head back to the classroom. Was it a dream? No, we are awake and happy.

The bad dreams of Ned's sudden plunge into aggression seem to be fading. It all gets better as he grows older, grows out of his adolescence, but there have been some losses, some promises not fulfilled. The baby who could make the letters of the alphabet writes very little better now. The three-year-old who eventually learned to play his little tune on the piano with two hands never touches the piano anymore. The boy who wanted to know all about everything in his beloved categories still cannot apply his knowledge in the real world. The twelve-year-old who quoted Shakespeare in Italy still requires a great deal of support to get through every day.

We have sent Ned some new clothes, hoping that he will be able to put his tearing days behind him. The packages arrive at Devereux, and Lorraine labels the garments and numbers them so we can keep track of which things fit well, which things Ned likes, and remember how to reorder them. This is a new all-out effort to see if Ned will stop tearing his clothes if he has things he really likes and that fit him perfectly. The word comes from Stan, who is usually with Ned when he dresses in the morning: "The new shoes got a big smile from Ned. He seems proud of his new clothes and was happy to model them for the class. He blushed a lot at all the compliments." And so far no tearing. Victory is in sight. A small victory, no doubt, but we'll take it.

Ned's grandmother is here for a visit, and we all go up to Devereux to see Ned. We drive onto the campus and head for the classroom where Ned is waiting for us. It is four years since Ned's grandmother has seen him, and we are hoping for a perfect day. A shy smile steals over Ned's face when he sees her. "Hi, Grammy." He is dressed in his new clothes, a boldly striped sweatshirt and soft denim trousers. Grammy goes off to the horses with Ned and the class. "He looked like a jockey on that horse," she reports excitedly, "with his striped shirt and red helmet. And he rides so beautifully, so naturally!" Ned poses for a snapshot with his grandmother. He is taller than she is, and he puts his arm around her. They are both smiling.

Lorraine calls with her weekly report. Ned is now completely off Mellaril and doing pretty well with his adjustment to the final reduction. He has some bad days, but his good ones are getting better. Everyone agrees that his language is improved, and last week he went to a movie, sat through the whole thing, and commented on the horses and the cowboys.

Ned's friends continue to come home with him, an ever-changing group. Staff comes and goes at Devereux, as it tends to do in such high-stress work. And the loss of a staff member can mean the loss of a friend for Ned. We always feel a pang when someone Ned likes particularly well leaves. It is so much more of a loss to him than the loss of a normal child's friend. But there seem to be phalanxes of enthusiastic, hard-working people willing to enter Ned's life, and he is fortunate that so many of them can see his good qualities and love him still, even when they have seen him at his worst.

John greets him in our driveway, "Hi, Ned."

"Hi, John." The two boys embrace.

"Kiss John," demands Ned.

"Let's shake hands instead," answers his brother.

Ned has been playing with a basketball at Devereux, and John would like to take him off to a nearby vacant lot where there is a basketball hoop, but we are not quite ready to have Ned out in public alone with John. Ned has made a lot of progress but we are cautious. Maybe next time. Soon.

We continue to have our dreams for Ned.

APPENDIX

Though no one mentioned in this book is a fictitious person, a few names as well as some identifying details have been changed where we thought it advisable. This is the story of one autistic child and his family, and where we have had failures, others may have succeeded; where we have found help and hope, others may have despaired. Nothing that was prescribed for Ned was intended for any other child, and the answers, therapies, and programs that were given us were for us alone. It is also well to remember that people and places and programs are always changing.

The following is a brief listing of some of the resources mentioned in this book:

The Devereux Foundation

For more information about the Devereux Foundation and the programs available through Devereux in eleven states, contact:

> The Devereux Foundation
> Box 400, 19 South Waterloo Road
> Devon, Pennsylvania 19333
> Phone: (215) 964-3050

The Institutes for the Achievement of Human Potential

If you wish to know more about the Institutes, contact:

> The Institutes for the Achievement of Human Potential
> 8801 Stenton Avenue
> Philadelphia, Pennsylvania 19118
> Phone: (215) 233-2050

There is also a great deal of information about the Institutes in Glenn Doman's books:

What to Do About Your Brain-Injured Child (Garden City, N.Y.: Doubleday, 1974)

How to Teach Your Baby to Read (New York: Random House, 1964)

Teach Your Baby Math (New York: Simon and Schuster, 1979)

How to Multiply Your Baby's Intelligence (Garden City, N.Y.: Doubleday, 1984)

Riding for the Handicapped

For information about horseback riding programs for the handicapped throughout the country, contact:

North American Riding for the Handicapped Association
P.O. Box 33150
Denver, Colorado 80233
Phone: (303) 452-1212

Autism

For general information about autism, contact:

Autism Society of America
Suite 1017
1234 Massachusetts Avenue, N.W.
Washington, D.C. 20005
Phone: (202) 783-0125

For insight into what it is like to be autistic, we recommend:

Emergence: Labeled Autistic (Navato, Calif.: Arena Press, 1986), by Temple Grandin and Margaret M. Scariano

Occupational Therapy

For information about occupational therapy using the sensory integration approach, contact:

Sensory Integration International
1402 Cravens Avenue
Torrance, California 90501

or

American Occupational Therapy Association
1383 Picard Drive
Rockville, Maryland 20850-4375

Other Resources

Edward R. Ritvo, M.D., and B. J. Freeman, Ph.D.
University of California at Los Angeles
Neuropsychiatric Institute and Hospital
760 Westwood Plaza
Los Angeles, California 90024

Robert L. Koegel, Ph.D.
Autism Research Center
Professor and Director
Department of Speech and Hearing Sciences
University of California at Santa Barbara
Santa Barbara, California 93106

Paul Millard Hardy, M.D.
Neuropsychiatrist at New England Medical Center
Assistant Professor of Neurology & Psychiatry
Tufts University School of Medicine
Department of Neurology
Box 314
750 Washington Street
Boston, Massachusetts 02111

Jay Nolan Center
Programs for the Developmentally Handicapped
26841 Ruether Avenue
Canyon Country, California 93151

INDEX